The New York Times

CHANGING PERSPECTIVES

Immigration

THE NEW YORK TIMES EDITORIAL STAFF

Published in 2019 by New York Times Educational Publishing
in association with The Rosen Publishing Group, Inc.
29 East 21st Street, New York, NY 10010

Contains material from The New York Times and is reprinted by permission. Copyright © 2019 The New York Times. All rights reserved.

Rosen Publishing materials copyright © 2019 The Rosen Publishing Group, Inc. All rights reserved. Distributed exclusively by Rosen Publishing.

First Edition

The New York Times
Alex Ward: Editorial Director, Book Development
Brenda Hutchings: Senior Photo Editor/Art Buyer
Phyllis Collazo: Photo Rights/Permissions Editor
Heidi Giovine: Administrative Manager

Rosen Publishing
Greg Tucker: Creative Director
Brian Garvey: Art Director
Megan Kellerman: Managing Editor
Carolyn DeCarlo: Editor

Cataloging-in-Publication Data

Names: New York Times Company.
Title: Immigration / edited by the New York Times editorial staff.
Description: New York : The New York Times Educational Publishing, 2019. | Series: Changing perspectives | Includes glossary and index.
Identifiers: ISBN 9781642820256 (pbk.) | ISBN 9781642820249 (library bound) | ISBN 9781642820232 (ebook)
Subjects: LCSH: Immigrants—United States—Juvenile literature. | United States—Emigration and immigration—Juvenile literature. | United States—Emigration and immigration—Government policy—Juvenile literature. | Illegal aliens—United States—Juvenile literature.
Classification: LCC JV6450.I464 2019 | DDC 304.8'73—dc23

Manufactured in the United States of America

On the cover: A Border Patrol agent at the fence along the border between the United States and Mexico on the outskirts of Nogales, Arizona; Thomas Munita for The New York Times.

Contents

8 Introduction

CHAPTER 1

A Nation of Immigrants

11 Immigration BY THE NEW YORK TIMES

13 Condemns Moves to Harass Aliens BY SAMUEL DICKSTEIN

16 Within the Gates BY OSCAR HANDLIN

18 Illegal Aliens' Health — and Ours BY THE NEW YORK TIMES

20 Employers Warned on Alien Hiring BY MARVINE HOWE

23 Don't Let the Amnesty Door Slam BY THE NEW YORK TIMES

25 For Elderly Immigrants, a Retirement Plan in U.S. BY ASHLEY DUNN

31 U.S. Official Is Indicted in Smuggling of Immigrants BY DANNY HAKIM

34 U.S. to Give Border Patrol Agents the Power to Deport Illegal Aliens BY RACHEL L. SWARNS

38 U.N. Report Cites Harassment of Immigrants Who Sought Asylum at American Airports BY RACHEL L. SWARNS

42 Safety Stings at Work Sites Will Be Halted BY STEVEN GREENHOUSE

43 Pink Slips at Disney. But First, Training Foreign Replacements. BY JULIA PRESTON

49 ICE Deportation Cases: Your Questions Answered
BY NIRAJ CHOKSHI AND VIVIAN YEE

54 Former ICE Lawyer Pleads Guilty to Stealing Immigrants' Identities to Spend $190,000 BY MATTHEW HAAG

CHAPTER 2

The Southern Border

56 Mexico Fears the Loss of America as a Safety Valve
BY LARRY ROHTER

60 Better Lives for Mexicans Cut Allure of Going North BY DAMIEN CAVE

71 Immigration; A Tale of Two Elections BY JULIÁN AGUILAR

72 American Children, Now Struggling to Adjust to Life in Mexico
BY DAMIEN CAVE

79 How One Sport Is Keeping a Language, and a Culture, Alive
BY WALTER THOMPSON-HERNÁNDEZ

85 Texas Banned 'Sanctuary Cities.' Some Police Departments Didn't Get the Memo. BY MANNY FERNANDEZ

CHAPTER 3

Children and Dreamers

89 I.N.S. Ruling Benefits Illegal Immigrant Children BY MARVINE HOWE

92 Mixed Scorecard for Immigrants' Children BY FORD FESSENDEN

94 For DACA Recipients, Losing Protection and Work Permits Is Just the Start BY CAITLIN DICKERSON

99 At Least 1,900 Immigrants Were Rejected Because of Mail Problems BY LIZ ROBBINS

102 DACA Participants Can Again Apply for Renewal, Immigration Agency Says BY MATT STEVENS

105 Fearing DACA's Return May Be Brief, Immigrants Rush to Renew BY LIZ ROBBINS AND MIRIAM JORDAN

110 Trump Says He Is Open to a Path to Citizenship for 'Dreamers' BY MAGGIE HABERMAN, KATIE ROGERS AND MICHAEL D. SHEAR

114 Most Americans Want Legal Status for 'Dreamers.' These People Don't. BY MIRIAM JORDAN

119 The Americans Left Behind by Deportation BY KARLA CORNEJO VILLAVICENCIO

CHAPTER 4

Individuals and Communities

123 Working to Help Irish Immigrants Stay, Legally BY MARVINE HOWE

128 With Affluent Chinese Moving In, a Press War Begins to Heat Up BY DAVID W. CHEN

131 Black Groups Seeking Asylum for a Teenager From Guinea BY JOHN FILES

133 Activists and ICE Face Off Over Detained Immigrant Leader BY LIZ ROBBINS

137 ICE Detained My Husband for Being an Activist BY AMY GOTTLIEB

140 President Trump, How Is This Man a Danger? BY NICHOLAS KRISTOF

CHAPTER 5

The Politics of Immigration

143 Court Ruling May Open Way for More Political Refugees
BY ROBERT PEAR

147 New Alliances and Attitudes on Aid BY CELIA W. DUGGER

151 U.S. Will Seek to Fingerprint Visas' Holders BY ERIC SCHMITT

154 New Policy Delays Visas for Specified Muslim Men
BY RAYMOND BONNER

157 Republican Split on Immigration Reflects Nation's Struggle
BY RACHEL L. SWARNS

161 The Immigration Debate; A Nation of Laws and of Immigrants
BY THE NEW YORK TIMES

167 '08 Candidates Weighing Consequences as They Take Sides on Immigration Plan BY MARC SANTORA

CHAPTER 6

Immigration and President Donald J. Trump

170 Once Routine, Immigration Check-Ins Are Now High Stakes
BY LIZ ROBBINS

176 Without New Laws or Walls, Trump Presses the Brake on Legal Immigration BY MIRIAM JORDAN

183 What Can the U.S. Learn From How Other Countries Handle Immigration? BY QUOCTRUNG BUI AND CAITLIN DICKERSON

189 Is America a 'Nation of Immigrants'? Immigration Agency Says No BY MIRIAM JORDAN

192 Did Melania Trump Merit an 'Einstein Visa'? Probably, Immigration Lawyers Say BY MIRIAM JORDAN

197 Immigration Agency Rails Against Oakland Mayor's Warning of Raids BY THOMAS FULLER

201 Trump Administration Sues California Over Immigration Laws
BY KATIE BENNER AND JENNIFER MEDINA

206 ICE Spokesman Resigns, Saying He Could No Longer Spread Falsehoods for Trump Administration BY JONAH ENGEL BROMWICH

209 Glossary
211 Media Literacy Terms
213 Media Literacy Questions
215 Citations
220 Index

Introduction

THE UNITED STATES is a nation founded by immigrants, and it would not be the country it is today without the influx of new voices and stories carried by the people arriving on its shores each year. Since its settlement by Europeans beginning in the late 15th century, this country has been viewed as "the land of opportunity," a place where people have the chance to improve their lives and achieve greatness — a concept known as the American dream.

For the first hundred-plus years of its existence, the United States had an open border policy, allowing anyone from anywhere in the world to enter the country and start a new life. This changed in 1921 with the introduction of the Emergency Quota Act, which limited the annual number of immigrants from certain countries. Since then, a vast range of laws restricting entry to the United States has been introduced with the intention of maintaining economic and social stability.

These restrictions have not deterred people from finding ways to enter the country and make it their home. Approximately one million people immigrate to the United States each year, and according to data from the Census Bureau, as of 2016 the immigrant population was 45.6 million, or 13.5 percent of U.S. residents. That makes America's immigrant population easily the largest in the world, at almost four times the size of Germany's immigrant population, which came in second.

The allure of the United States is so strong that many people who don't qualify for residence choose to enter the country illegally. Many of those who make it across the border live the rest of their lives in America without access to health insurance or benefits even though they pay U.S. taxes and contribute to society in a number

Miguel Cruz Jr., background, with Jorge Cruz in Southern California's San Fernando Valley. They are playing the traditional Oaxacan game of pelota mixteca, which serves as a network for an immigrant community spanning the West Coast.

of ways. This has become a hotly debated political issue, with one extreme arguing for the immediate deportation of all undocumented immigrants in order to protect the safety and well-being of American citizens, while the other side fights for the rights and interests of the immigrants and advocates for creating pathways to citizenship for them.

While public opinion on immigration is split, the fact remains that not only do immigrants benefit from relocating to America, but America also benefits from the skills and successes of the people who choose to make this nation their home. Many American icons were born in other countries and immigrated to the United States. America's first female secretary of state, Madeleine Albright, was born in Czechoslovakia. Action movie star and former governor of California Arnold Schwarzenegger grew up in Austria until moving to America at the age of 21. Nobel Prize-winning physicist Albert Einstein spent most of his life in Germany before immigrating to the United States in 1933 to avoid persecution from the Nazi Party. They all contributed greatly to society and became embodiments of the American dream. While current policies limiting entry into the United States provide stability for existing residents, it is impossible to tell what impact, positive or negative, they will have on the future of America.

CHAPTER 1

A Nation of Immigrants

America prides itself on being a nation of immigrants, yet relationships with newcomers to the country are not always positive. American citizens have been outwardly hostile toward people born in other countries trying to make a home in the United States. Historically, there have always been differing perspectives on immigration. This conflict has resulted in a system of laws and regulations that can be difficult for new arrivals to navigate. However, every year, hundreds of thousands of immigrants continue to arrive for reasons as varied as their backgrounds.

Immigration

BY THE NEW YORK TIMES | AUG. 26, 1890

THE TIDE OF IMMIGRATION continues to rise with somewhat striking eddies here and there. The monthly increases over 1889 of a few unimpressive thousands have swollen for the year already to over 29,000, or more than our regular army. On the other hand, the monthly decreases in arrivals from the British Kingdom have aggregated nearly 17,000. It will be interesting to notice whether the potato famine will again swell the diminishing Irish quota.

Doubtless the Czar's cruelty is reflected in the increase of Russian arrivals by 3,280. When he last attacked his Jews they flocked here by thousands, and a sorry lot they were. They were not only pitifully poor, but they were filthy and ungrateful and riotous, and altogether unwelcome guests. It is well to remember how our hospitality was abused, however ungracious it may seem to revive such memories, now that a similar experience seems at hand. We wonder for what special reason the Austrians are now leaving home in such growing numbers. There are almost as many more of them (15,331) as there are fewer Britons, and we are sorry that the Hungarian quota is just about doubled. The Italian arrivals here have increased themselves by the difference between 40,646 and 17,224. But the greatest percentage of increase is in the Poles. Their arrivals have almost quadrupled to 40,646. On the other hand, the arrivals of Germans, Swedes, and Swiss are lessening.

This tendency of our most desirable recruits to stay at home, and of our most ignorant, turbulent, and unreconstructible immigrants to increase, has been noted before and may yet have serious results.

Condemns Moves to Harass Aliens

BY SAMUEL DICKSTEIN | JUNE 30, 1935

WASHINGTON — The law-abiding citizens in the United States should not be handicapped, in these difficult times of economic readjustment, by threats of wholesale and mandatory deportations and compulsory naturalization.

Assertions have been made in print and by voice which would have the general public believe there are now in the United States from 6,000,000 to 20,000,000 aliens and that of these aliens from 3,500,000 to 10,000,000 are now here illegally and subject to deportation. It has also been proposed that all aliens now unlawfully here should be immediately deported and that all aliens who are legally here should become citizens within a year.

All of these statements are so fantastic and are such exaggerations that I feel all right-thinking American people should be given, without delay, an answer with authoritative information from trustworthy sources.

OFFICIAL FIGURES.

Following a most careful examination of the records of the Census Bureau, of the records of the Immigration and Naturalization Service and of other sources of reliable information, Daniel W. MacCormack, Commissioner of Immigration and Naturalization, recently told our committee during open public hearings that the total number of foreign born persons now in the United States, other than those who have become citizens or those who have filed their declarations of intention to become citizens, or those minors who will become citizens upon the naturalization of parents with declarations of intention, is not in excess of 3,403,000.

Colonel MacCormack at the same hearings also stated that he was compelled to the conclusion that it is extremely unlikely that there are now as many as 100,000 aliens who are here illegally and subject to deportation under existing laws.

The Kerr bill, which is now awaiting consideration on the floor of the House, is primarily a legislative measure to enable the more effective and humanitarian administration of our deportation laws, but the inevitable results of its enactment will be to reduce the alien population of our country and to further restrict hereafter both legal and illegal immigration.

SPECIAL CASES.

An interdepartmental committee, made up of representatives of three government departments — Justice, State and Labor — will be authorized to study certain cases involving aliens who are in the non-criminal classes — that is, aliens whose only offense may be a technical violation of the Immigration Law but for which there is no criminal penalty provided other than deportation, and in these cases exercise limited discretion to adjust the status of certain of these aliens in a humane manner, calculated to preserve the unity of homes honorably established on American soil and to prevent American-born minor children from becoming orphans in their native land.

The Kerr bill grants no discretionary power to adjust the status of any alien whose deportation is mandatory under existing law on grounds that the alien has been convicted of a crime involving moral turpitude, or is deportable as an anarchist or Communist, or is deportable on account of any violation of State or Federal laws regarding the importation or sale or distribution of narcotics, or who is not of a good moral character.

Deportations will be greater in number because there are four classes added to the aliens subject to deportation that are not covered by existing law; these include the habitual criminal, the racketeer, the gunman, the alien smuggler of aliens and violators of State narcotic laws. Apprehensions of aliens subject to deportation and temporary detention of them without warrant will legally enable immigration officials more efficiently to get aliens who now escape and are lost before the issuance of a lawful warrant can be secured.

DEDUCTIONS FROM QUOTAS.

Fewer foreign-born persons who have never before been here will arrive as quota immigrants because the number of all aliens who have been permitted by the interdepartmental committee to remain will be deducted from the quota of the countries from which they originally came here. Skilled agriculturists will no longer have the preference status which they now have under the quotas.

This bill will clean up a great deal of the injustice that our present inflexible deportation law has made mandatory. These inhuman practices have been known for years by thoughtful students of the operation of our immigration laws, and Congress has been urged for a long time to legislate the necessary remedies. The Kerr bill will bring the needed relief and will thereby increase the wholesome respect for our immigration laws. The Kerr bill should be speedily made law, and I will do all I possibly can to bring that about.

Within the Gates

BY OSCAR HANDLIN | FEB. 19, 1950

A QUARTER-CENTURY has gone by since the great reversal in American attitudes toward immigration. That interval has given us the perspective and the material for re-evaluating the new policy of restriction, based on racial quotas, which in 1924 supplanted the traditional policy of open gates. Examining the experience of these twenty-five years, Mr. Bernard, director of the National Committee on Immigration Policy, and his colleagues analyze the consequences of restriction.

The quota legislation of 1924 was a product of prejudice and fear; it took no account of the possible effects of restriction on the national economic interests or on the international position of the United States. To hold now to these anachronistic statutes is a danger and dubious luxury we can ill afford.

The arguments in this volume are hardly controvertible in scholarly terms. Here is an array of data that should put at rest the old uneasinesses as to whether immigrants would adapt themselves to American society. A survey of the records of naturalization, of literacy, of participation in our wars, of criminality, pauperism and health, demonstrates the completeness of the adjustment.

Two succinct chapters on demographic trends reveal the clear probability of a decline in the size of American population in the next few decades if there is no further immigration, with damaging strategic consequences in view of the certain continued rise in the population of Russia and Eastern Europe. Finally, there is an outline of the effects on the future expansion of our economy, of the relationship of immigration to unemployment and depressions.

The concluding recommendations of the volume are moderate, too moderate indeed for the tastes of this reviewer. Mr. Bernard urges that the present level of admissions be maintained or enlarged, that a flexibility provision be introduced so that unfilled quotas will not be wasted, and that a Congressional committee study the quota system itself.

Here are the materials for dispelling the prejudices behind our present immigration policy. The real question is: Can facts and logic dispel fears born of bias? It might have been as well had the compilers of this book been less temperate, labeled the quota system for what it is, and called for its immediate repeal.

MR. HANDLIN, ASSOCIATE PROFESSOR OF HISTORY AT HARVARD, WROTE "BOSTON'S IMMIGRANTS: A STUDY OF ACCULTURATION."

Illegal Aliens' Health — and Ours

BY THE NEW YORK TIMES | AUG. 10, 1986

SHOULD UNDOCUMENTED ALIENS be eligible for Medicaid? Yes, says a Federal district judge in Brooklyn. No, says a New Jersey Congressman worried about the cost. The concern is understandable, but this social service expenditure is cost effective as well as humane.

Across the country, the burden of providing health care to undocumented aliens falls mostly on public hospitals. Many such patients are poor enough to qualify for Medicaid, the health insurance for the indigent funded jointly by the Federal and local governments. But a 1973 regulation bars Federal Medicaid help for them.

A class-action challenge on behalf of illegal aliens in New York resulted in a recent decision striking down the 1973 rule. Federal District Judge Charles Sifton found it insupportable because, he said, the 1966 law authorizing Medicaid contains "no express restrictions on alien eligibility."

Representative Matthew Rinaldo of New Jersey is therefore sponsoring an amendment to the House budget reconciliation bill that would close the loophole. He would expressly prohibit the Federal share of Medicaid coverage for undocumented aliens, thereby throwing the full burden onto localities.

The approach is shortsighted. Reduced Medicaid help for the undocumented means that they defer medical care for as long as possible, then show up for treatment at already overburdened locally run public hospitals and clinics. New York City, for example, now absorbs an estimated $25 million in unreimbursed Medicaid payments for illegal aliens. Fully half of the patients are pregnant women who do not seek help until just before delivery. Assuring them adequate prenatal care would cost less than providing treatment for their babies, who, having been born here, are citizens eligible for Medicaid.

Additional savings to the city might result from the immunization of young children, proper treatment for the aged, blind and disabled and the shift of patients from acute care to nursing homes or home care available under Medicaid.

Senator Moynihan argues that all undocumented aliens should be entitled to Medicaid since illegal immigration reflects the Federal Government's failure to control the borders. That may overstate the issue, but the practical case seems irrefutable for helping all who are pregnant, young children, aged, blind or otherwise disabled.

A Federal tax dollar spent to give them rational health care would automatically save many more tax dollars eventually necessary to compensate for their neglect.

Employers Warned on Alien Hiring

BY MARVINE HOWE | AUG. 9, 1987

A SENIOR IMMIGRATION OFFICIAL reassured the managers of a curtain factory in Long Island City the other day that he had come to explain the new immigration law's provisions on employer sanctions, "not enforce them."

"No firm will be cited or fined until we have made an information visit," said John O'Malley, senior special agent for the Immigration and Naturalization Service. He warned, however, that action would soon be taken against "blatant violators."

The I.N.S. is currently engaged in a widespread door-to-door campaign to inform employers about the Immigration and Reform Control Act, which went into effect June 1, prohibiting the hiring of illegal aliens and providing stiff penalties for continued violations.

Thus far, there have been no citations, fines or arrests for violations under the new immigration law in the Eastern Region, according to Carol Chasse, the I.N.S. assistant commissioner for Employer and Labor Relations for the region, which includes the East Coast to the District of Columbia and Puerto Rico.

Since mid-June, I.N.S. investigative staff and border patrols have been devoting about 50 percent of their time to the Information and Education Program, Ms. Chasse said. Nearly 5,000 on-site visits to employers have been made in the Eastern Region.

The second phase of the program will be audit visits, based on "neutrally produced lists" and should begin sometime in the fall, according to Mr. O'Malley. The third phase will be investigation, coming generally as a result of the audits and complaints.

But fines could be imposed almost immediately on "blatant violators," Mr. O'Malley said, referring to employers who had either openly refused to comply with the new law, evaded information visits or were subject to strong complaints.

In the stark, white-washed conference room at Karpel Curtains, the personnel manager and three supervisors voiced the main concerns of employers trying to comply with the new immigration law. Their questions focused on the calendar and paperwork required for the new I-9 form and the responsibility for fraudulent documents.

INCREASE IN FINES

"We're asking employers to do two things with the I-9 form: verify the employee's identity and authorization to work in this country," Mr. O'Malley said. He outlined the procedure now required for all new employees, including American citizens, with the exception of independent contractors, self-employed or people hired for domestic work on a sporadic basis.

Employers are not required to fill out I-9 forms for employees hired before Nov. 6, 1986, when the immigration law was signed, he said. Employers have until Sept. 1, 1987, to fill out I-9 forms for all employees, hired after Nov. 6, 1986, and still in their employ by June 1, 1987. As of June 1, 1987, employers must fill out I-9 forms for all employees, within three business days of hire, with a possible 21-day extension.

Mr. O'Malley noted that employers continuing to hire unauthorized workers after a warning citation, risk fines of up to $2,000 per employee for the first violation, $5,000 for the second violation and $10,000 for subsequent violations. In addition, employers failing to keep records of I-9 forms face fines of up to $1,000 for each employee.

Discussing documents required for the I-9, Mr. O'Malley pointed out that some American citizens, particularly teenagers, were having problems. He said the I.N.S. would accept school, medical or parental identification for people under 16 and working papers from the Department of Education for youths 16 and 17 years old.

On the question of fake documents, Mr. O'Malley said that employers were "not expected to use a microscope but the documentation must look reasonably genuine."

Other problems were raised during an I.N.S. informational visit to the Manhattan advertising agency, Bozell, Jacobs, Kenyon & Eckhardt, which hires hundreds of people temporarily as talent each year and scores of freelance writers and producers.

Would artists and freelance people, sometimes hired for only one day, have to fill out the I-9 forms? asked Armand Fabiano, director of the firm's Human Resources Operations. He was concerned about the cost of the three-day grace period for filling out the forms. Couldn't an employment agency or the Screen Actors Guild take care of the I-9 forms?

Agencies may handle verification procedures, but employers continue to bear the responsibility for compliance with the law, Mr. O'Malley said. He added that the I.N.S. has begun discussions with the Screen Actors Guild about the problem.

"How do we ask Frank Sinatra to fill out an I-9 form?" one of the supervisors asked.

Don't Let the Amnesty Door Slam

BY THE NEW YORK TIMES | NOV. 3, 1987

CONGRESS PASSED the Immigration Reform and Control Act last year to make it harder for new illegal aliens to stay in this country — and easier for old ones. The act provided amnesty for aliens who had been here since at least 1982. But they were given only 12 months to apply, and even that time has been constricted. Fairness alone would impel Congress to keep the legalization door open an additional year, to May 4, 1989.

The first goal was to deter illegal immigrants by forbidding employers to hire them. Early evidence indicates that this goal is being met. The second goal was to bring out of the shadows hundreds of thousands of aliens who have lived in this country illegally, and furtively, for years. This goal has been less well met.

Many of the eligible aliens need more time to apply. The Immigration and Naturalization Service did not start taking applications until May 5. So far, across the nation, less than a million illegals have applied for legalized status; less than 50,000 are from the New York area. I.N.S. legalization offices are operating at 50 percent capacity in the West and only 20 percent in the East.

If these rates continue, the program will legalize far fewer aliens than anticipated. Also, the approval process has been painfully slow. Only 75,000 amnesty requests have been granted. The most effective way to spur applications is to decide cases and let beneficiaries spread the word.

It comes as no surprise that the Immigration Service is still ironing the wrinkles out of this massive effort. There have been computer problems. National and regional information campaigns take time to develop. Outreach and networking have been inadequate: it takes vast effort to penetrate thousands of alien enclaves. In addition, clarification is needed for regulations about length of continuous residence, proof of employment and policies regarding the protection of family members.

Aliens, some daunted by language, have hung back. Some don't understand the new law. Some fear, incorrectly, that even if one member of a family is eligible for amnesty, a spouse, parents or children could be deported based on information on the application form. There must be time for accurate information to be disseminated and digested, and for understanding and trust to develop. The Immigration Service is, after all, the agency that deports people.

The Service has worked hard to make the amnesty program work. By extending legalization to May 4, 1989, Congress would insure that it does.

For Elderly Immigrants, a Retirement Plan in U.S.

BY ASHLEY DUNN | APRIL 16, 1995

IT WAS IN THE CHAOTIC din of a Chinatown garment factory that 74-year-old Ho Yin-peng discovered a better way to survive than snipping loose threads from clothing at 5 cents a dress.

Her coworkers told her that even though she lived with her son, she could qualify for the Federal welfare program known as Supplemental Security Income if she was over 65 and had been in this country for more than three years.

So after she passed the third anniversary of her residence in the United States in 1991, she applied and soon began receiving $280 a month, far more than she made in the factory at $40 a week. She has not worked since.

"It's not enough for living expenses, but its more than when I was working," said Mrs. Ho, who now shares a small apartment with a friend in Chinatown. "Everyone knows about this."

Created in the early 1970's to bolster the incomes of retirees who did not receive enough in Social Security, the Supplemental Security Income program is increasingly being sought out by elderly immigrants new to this country.

Unlike regular Social Security, which is a contributory insurance plan based on how long people worked and how much they made before retirement, S.S.I. is a welfare program for all citizens or resident immigrants who meet certain requirements of age, income or disability.

The number of elderly immigrants enrolled in the program has increased fivefold over the last 12 years. Now, more than a quarter of immigrants over 65 — and in some immigrant populations, almost half — receive S.S.I., at an annual cost of $2 billion.

By comparison, less than 10 percent of elderly United States citizens are in the program.

S.S.I. has, in fact, become something akin to a retirement system for elderly immigrants, who in many cases come from countries that have meager or nonexistent retirement systems. It is not believed to be the magnet that draws them here, since most come to join their children or other relatives who moved here first. But the S.S.I. system, which has become widely known among immigrants in the United States and abroad, is the one welfare program that immigrants use more heavily than do native-born Americans. Illegal immigrants are ineligible.

"The American dream is no longer to start at the bottom and work your way up," said Daniel Stein, executive director of the Federation for American Immigration Reform. "It's to transfer your assets to your children and get on S.S.I. as fast as you can."

But advocates for immigrants counter that the program is necessary to protect one of the most vulnerable groups in American society, elderly immigrants who come to join their children and later find that their families will not or cannot support them.

"I was hoping my children would take care of me when I got old," Mrs. Ho said. "But they all have their own families. It's the American style."

Under the Republican-backed welfare overhaul under consideration in Washington, Mrs. Ho and thousands of other immigrants between ages 65 and 75 would lose their eligibility for S.S.I. But those over 75, who are about half the immigrants collecting S.S.I., would remain eligible — an exemption, the Republicans say, that is based on compassion for the elderly poor.

The growing population of elderly immigrants collecting S.S.I. is partly explained by the surge in immigration over the past decade. But while immigration has doubled, the number of elderly immigrants enrolled in the program has increased fivefold, to 440,000 today from 91,900 in 1982.

Norman S. Matloff, a professor of computer science at University of California at Davis who did an analysis of census data concerning immigrants receiving S.S.I. benefits, said a reason may be simply that the benefits are available and easy to receive.

"Everybody knows that this is free money," Mr. Matloff said. "The knowledge about this overseas has just mushroomed."

An analysis of 1990 census information conducted for The New York Times by Andrew Beveridge, a sociologist at Queens College, shows that about 20 percent of the immigrants receiving the supplemental benefits actually live in households with incomes above $50,000 a year. The national median income for households of five people, the average size of immigrant households, is $37,000.

The Republican welfare changes, which have passed the House but have not yet been taken up in the Senate, would exclude only about a third of those elderly immigrants in households making more than $50,000 a year, Mr. Beveridge's study found.

The S.S.I. eligibility requirements are for incomes of less than about $450 a month, depending on the state, and liquid assets of less than $2,000, but the rules do not take into account the wealth of the applicant's children.

"Someone could be living with Donald Trump and if they don't have a nickel to their name, they're going to qualify," said Thomas Margenau, a spokesman for the Social Security Administration.

Most immigrants are sponsored by family members to come to this country. In theory, their sponsors are financially responsible for them until they become citizens. Their sponsors are required by the Government to sign an affidavit, promising that the immigrants will not become public charges.

But the affidavits have been ruled legally unenforceable and most immigrants can apply for welfare after they have lived in the country long enough regardless of how much their sponsors make.

Until 1994, elderly immigrants could qualify as "permanent resident aliens" and become eligible for S.S.I. after three years in this country. Government statistics show that a quarter of them applied within months of passing the three-year mark. But the growth in the number of applications pushed the Social Security Administration to change the residency requirement last year to five years.

Supplemental Security Income was established in 1972 by amendments to the Social Security Act and took effect in 1974. It replaced an old system of Federal grants to the states for old-age assistance and aid to the blind and disabled.

Over the years, the number of citizens in the program has declined, dropping by a half million just since 1982, largely because more people are covered by other types of retirement incomes. In that same period, the proportion of elderly immigrants receiving S.S.I. has increased to more than 30 percent from 6 percent.

Mexicans make up the biggest group of immigrants receiving Supplemental Security Income. But compared with the size of the Mexican immigrant population in the United States, their usage rate is lower than that of many other nationalities.

Laotians are the most likely to be collecting S.S.I., with nearly two-thirds of those over 65 enrolled in the program. Among nonrefugee groups, Koreans have the highest usage rate, with slightly less than half of those over 65 enrolled, according to the analysis of 1990 census data by Mr. Beveridge.

Advocates for immigrants say it is only natural that more immigrants are relying on the program, since they generally have worked a shorter time in this country and are often employed in low-paying factory or service jobs, which leaves them ineligible for Social Security or receiving only low benefits.

Amelia Jacoma, who is 68, came to the United States from Ecuador in 1957 and spent three decades working as a seamstress in New York City. She paid her income taxes and contributed to Social Security, and owned her own home in the Bronx.

But the most she ever made was $240 a week and, after retiring, her Social Security check came to just $380 a month.

S.S.I., which provides benefits based on other other income and varies from case to case, gives her an extra $130 a month — the difference, she said, between poverty and survival.

"I worked all my life in this country and that's all I got," she said.

The program also has been savior for many elderly immigrants trapped in the modern reality of dispersed families and changing traditions.

Mrs. Ho, an ethnic Chinese from the Malaysian city of Melaka, came to the United States to settle in 1988 when she was 67, in part to help take care of her daughter's young children.

But as her grandchildren grew older, she said she became more a burden to her own children.

With her S.S.I. benefits, she was able to move out on her own. Now she pays $100 a month for a small room off Hester Street with just enough space for a bed and plastic lawn chair, her only furniture. She eats lunch at a nearby senior citizens' center for 50 cents a meal and cooks a simple dinner each night.

The faded green walls of her room are adorned with calendars of movie stars or Chinese gods that the restaurants and grocery stores in Chinatown give away. All her other possessions fit in a few boxes and suitcases at the foot of her bed.

"It's comfortable enough for me here," she said. "If I was in Malaysia, I would have no money, no home."

Mr. Matloff, whose study included interviews with ethnic Chinese in California, said he believed that the ease of receiving S.S.I. has helped destroy old traditions of caring for the aged.

"It's become an easy alternative to working out family difficulties," he said.

Maria Theresa R., a 70-year-old immigrant from Ecuador who refused to be identified by her full name because she was embarrassed by her plight, said she was originally sent by her children to America because they did not have the means to care for her in their homeland any longer.

For a year and a half she lived with a son in the Bronx, but eventually left after family disputes.

She survives now on $544 in S.S.I. benefits each month and 50-cent meals at a nearby senior citizens' center in the East Tremont section of the Bronx.

She cannot go back to Ecuador, nor has she anyone in the United States to care for her. "This is my home," she said as she picked at her plate of rice and chicken in the center's dining hall. "There is really nothing else for me now."

U.S. Official Is Indicted in Smuggling of Immigrants

BY DANNY HAKIM | APRIL 22, 2003

FEDERAL PROSECUTORS here indicted an immigration official at the Department of Homeland Security and two other people today, accusing them of conspiring to smuggle 130 illegal immigrants into the country from Lebanon and Yemen over five years.

"Immigration fraud cases like this potentially pose a threat to national security," said Jeffrey G. Collins, the United States Attorney for the Eastern District of Michigan, "and that's why we are vigorously prosecuting the case, including prosecuting an employee of the entity that was supposed to protect us."

Mr. Collins said that more than half of the illegal immigrants had been found and that none of those had been determined to have discernable connections to terrorism. They entered the United States between 1998 and October 2002.

There was little clarity, though, regarding those illegal immigrants who had not yet been found. Federal agents are looking for them, Mr. Collins said, adding that prosecutors would "make a determination on a case-by-case basis whether or not they should be criminally charged or be removed from the country."

Janice Halstead, 59, of Detroit, was indicted for bribery, two counts of conspiracy to smuggle illegal immigrants into the United States, and several counts of attempted alien smuggling. Ms. Halstead, who worked for the Immigration and Naturalization Service and then for the Department of Homeland Security when the immigration agency became a part of it, received $3,000 to $5,000 in cash, a bedroom set, jewelry and other gifts, the indictment and Mr. Collins said.

The overall value of the goods and cash was not disclosed.

Ms. Halstead, reached at home after being released on bond, said she was not guilty. She has not formally entered a plea.

"I think I probably made the wrong person mad," she said, adding that she did know one of the other defendants, Zoha Madarani, but not the other, Salah Al-Solihi.

Ms. Madarani, 38, of Dearborn, Mich., and Mr. Al-Solihi, 45, of New York, were indicted for conspiracy to smuggle illegal immigrants into the United States and charges related to immigrant smuggling.

Ms. Madarani and Mr. Al-Solihi could not be found, and officials did not say if they were citizens or foreigners.

The indictments, which were unsealed today, stem from two similar cases involving federal grand juries in Detroit and Flint, both part of the Eastern District of Michigan.

Ms. Madarani was indicted in federal court in Detroit, and Mr. Al-Solihi in Flint. Both grand juries indicted Ms. Halstead.

In the case from the Flint grand jury, Mr. Al-Solihi is accused of instructing foreigners to obtain false passports with false names. Ms. Halstead is accused of validating them with an official stamp, while Mr. Al-Solihi is accused of sending them overseas, where they were used by foreigners to enter the country.

In the case from the Detroit grand jury, Ms. Madarani is accused of providing Ms. Halstead with the names and photographs of people living outside of the country who were not eligible to enter legally. The indictment says the two women conspired to provide the inadmissible immigrants with false documents.

Ms. Madarani owns a consulting business that helps potential immigrants, according to the indictment.

"The case is very disturbing because it represents a violation of public trust," Mr. Collins said.

Edward Dyner, special agent in charge of the Justice Department's office of inspector general, said in a statement: "Department of Justice employees are not for sale. The inspector general's office takes seriously any allegations against department employees and will thoroughly investigate them."

If convicted, Ms. Halstead faces up to 22 years in prison and $750,000 in fines from the Detroit case and up to 65 years in prison and $1.5 million in the Flint case. Ms. Madarani could receive up to 20 years in prison and a $750,000 fine; Mr. Al-Solihi faces 65 years in prison and $1.5 million in fines.

U.S. to Give Border Patrol Agents the Power to Deport Illegal Aliens

BY RACHEL L. SWARNS | AUG. 11, 2004

CITING CONCERNS ABOUT TERRORISTS crossing the nation's borders, the Department of Homeland Security said on Tuesday that it planned to give border patrol agents sweeping new powers to deport illegal aliens from the frontiers with Mexico and Canada without providing them the opportunity to make their case before an immigration judge.

The move, which will take effect this month, represents a broad expansion of the authority of the thousands of law enforcement agents who patrol the nation's borders. Until now, border patrol agents typically delivered undocumented immigrants to the custody of the immigration courts, where judges determined whether they should be deported or remain in the United States.

Domestic security officials described the deportation process in immigration courts — which hear asylum claims and other appeals to remain in the country — as sluggish and cumbersome, saying illegal immigrants often wait for more than a year before being deported while straining the capacity of detention centers and draining critical resources. Under the new system, immigrants will typically be deported within eight days of their apprehension, officials said.

The Illegal Immigration and Reform Responsibility Act of 1996 authorized the agency to deport certain groups of illegal immigrants without judicial oversight, but until now it had permitted only officials at airports and seaports to do so.

The new rule will apply to illegal immigrants caught within 100 miles of the Mexican and Canadian borders who have spent up to 14 days within the United States. Officials said the border agents would not focus on deporting Mexicans and Canadians, who will still, for the most part, have their cases heard in immigration court. The agents will concentrate instead on immigrants from other countries. In fiscal year 2003, about 37,000 immigrants from countries other than Mexico and Canada — primarily from Central America — were arrested along the Southwest border.

Officials said that the new plan would help deter illegal immigration, speed deportations and address issues of border security.

"There is a concern that as we tighten the security of our ports of entry through our biometric checks that there will be more opportunity or more effort made by terrorists to enter our country through our vast land borders," Asa Hutchinson, the undersecretary for border security at the Department of Homeland Security, said at a news conference.

The decision was hailed by officials who have long complained that the nation's porous borders represent a serious threat to national security. But it prompted a flurry of criticism from advocates for immigrants who feared that the new system lacked adequate safeguards to ensure that people fleeing persecution, Americans lacking paperwork or other travelers with legitimate grounds to be in the United States would not be improperly deported.

Mr. Hutchinson said that border agents would be trained in asylum law and that immigrants who showed a credible fear of persecution would be provided hearings before immigration judges, not returned to hostile governments. "That right," he said of the right to apply for asylum, "is very important."

Homeland security officials said that the training would last for several days and that agents would begin their new duties in Tucson and Laredo, Tex.

Advocates for immigrants said they feared mistakes would be made when hastily trained border agents decide who should be deported and who should not. Complaints about improper deportations have already been reported at some airports and seaports.

"We're very concerned that we may see the mistaken deportations of refugees, citizens and other legitimate visitors," said Eleanor Acer, director of the asylum program of Human Rights First, an advocacy group. "For refugees, it could be a life or death sentence."

The officials also announced plans on Tuesday to allow the roughly seven million Mexicans who carry border crossing cards — which let them visit the United States for three consecutive days — to visit for up to 30 days at a time using the same card.

Mr. Hutchinson said the announcements were part of a two-pronged strategy. "We want to send a clear message that those individuals who follow legal immigration rules will benefit, while those who choose to break our nation's immigration laws will be promptly removed from the U.S.," he said.

Evelyn Nazro, a spokeswoman for the Alliance for Security and Trade, a coalition that represents public officials and business leaders in Texas, described the shift as "a step in the right direction."

But Ms. Nazro said that many business executives and public officials would like Mexican visitors to be allowed to stay for six months, as Canadian visitors are. "It's long been a real issue that Mexicans had such limitations on their visas," she said.

Discussions about accelerating deportations along the nation's borders have been held for some time. Tuesday's announcement is the second time that the government has expanded the "expedited removal" process since the Sept. 11 attacks.

In November 2002, the government said it was extending the process of deportations without judicial review for undocumented immigrants at airports to those at seaports.

Officials said that Mexicans were not the focus of the new deportation efforts because most undocumented Mexicans choose to return after being caught. But Mr. Hutchinson said that Mexicans who smuggle immigrants and who repeatedly violate immigration laws would also be subject to the speedy deportations.

In fiscal year 2003, about 43,000 immigrants were swiftly deported without scrutiny from immigration judges. The new rules could nearly double that figure, homeland security statistics suggest. Officials said they would observe Tucson and Laredo, where roughly 3,050 agents will assume their new duties, before applying the process to other border regions. "After we get it going, we'll begin discussions about expanding it," a spokeswoman for the Department of Homeland Security said.

U.N. Report Cites Harassment of Immigrants Who Sought Asylum at American Airports

BY RACHEL L. SWARNS | AUG. 13, 2004

A CONFIDENTIAL REPORT conducted by the United Nations in cooperation with the Department of Homeland Security has found that airport inspectors with the power to summarily deport illegal immigrants have sometimes intimidated and handcuffed travelers fleeing persecution, discouraged some from seeking political asylum and often lacked an understanding of asylum law.

Homeland Security officials say they have responded to the problems identified in the report, which was completed late last year and obtained this week by The New York Times. But the study highlights the challenges facing the department as it grants Border Patrol agents sweeping new powers to deport illegal immigrants from the borders with Mexico and Canada without providing them the opportunity to make their case before an immigration judge.

Until now, Border Patrol agents typically delivered illegal immigrants to the custody of the immigration courts, where judges determined whether they should be deported or remain in the United States. Homeland Security officials, who announced the policy shift this week, said border agents would be trained before deporting illegal immigrants to ensure that asylum seekers and legitimate travelers were not mistakenly sent home.

In its report, the United Nations high commissioner for refugees commended the department for working to safeguard people fleeing persecution, noting that most airport inspectors properly identified asylum seekers and correctly referred them for further interviews to ensure that their cases would be heard by an immigration judge. But the United Nations noted that problems remained at American airports — where summary deportations have occurred since 1997 — even after inspectors received training about the importance of protecting asylum seekers.

The report found that inspectors at airports often failed to provide certified translators for asylum seekers who did not speak English, improperly notified consulates about the identity and detention of immigrants seeking asylum, and in 14 cases mistakenly concluded that travelers who expressed a credible fear of persecution were not entitled to apply for asylum.

Joung-ah Ghedini, a spokeswoman for the United Nations high commissioner for refugees, expressed concern about the expansion of summary deportations to the nation's borders. Ms. Ghedini said the United Nations wanted to know more about the training of border agents to ensure that asylum seekers were protected.

"What we're concerned about is that we don't know many of the details of what will happen when the expansion of expedited removal is implemented at the borders," said Ms. Ghedini, who declined to discuss the details of the report.

Commissioner Robert C. Bonner, who heads the customs and border protection unit at the Department of Homeland Security, said the training for Border Patrol agents would protect asylum seekers, who are entitled to have their cases reviewed by an immigration judge if they express a credible fear of persecution.

Mr. Bonner said the training curriculum had been approved by the department's civil rights office and would begin next week in Tucson and the following week in Laredo, Tex., the first places along the border where summary deportations are expected to begin. Supervisors will receive two days of training and Border Patrol agents will each typically receive a one-day, eight-hour training session over the next few weeks, officials said.

"We want to make sure we roll this out and do this right and appropriately," Mr. Bonner said in an interview. "It's our responsibility to make sure that there's adequate training, including any refresher training that might be necessary, so that persons that do potentially have asylum claims are appropriately referred. It's certainly something we take very seriously."

In conducting its study, United Nations officials reviewed more than 300 case files; interviewed dozens of inspectors, supervisors and asylum officers; and sat in on more than 100 interviews with asylum seekers at airports in New York, Newark, Miami and Los Angeles.

The Department of Homeland Security granted the United Nations access to internal documents, staff members and asylum seekers on the condition that the report not be released to the public after it was completed in late October. The study was provided to The New York Times by a person unaffiliated with the United Nations who was concerned about the government's plan to expand summary deportations to the country's land borders.

In its report, the United Nations discovered that many inspectors held negative views of asylum seekers, viewing them as frauds trying to enter the United States under false pretenses. Such attitudes, the report concluded, resulted in instances where inspectors intimidated asylum seekers or treated them with derision.

At Kennedy International Airport in New York, asylum seekers were routinely handcuffed and restrained with belly chains and leg restraints. In one instance there, a Liberian asylum seeker was ordered to strip naked to determine whether he had scars consistent with torture. The inspectors then allegedly ridiculed him, using racial and sexual taunts.

"With regard to treatment of asylum-seekers, the overuse of restraints, such as at J.F.K., and the frequency of negative, and at times hostile, attitudes towards asylum-seekers is of significant concern," the report said.

The study also described two instances in which inspectors encouraged asylum seekers not to pursue asylum claims. "These incidents, even if isolated, are extremely troubling given the risks of returning someone to a country of possible persecution," it said.

Ms. Ghedini said Homeland Security officials had addressed some issues in the report, including making efforts to improve training. "Generally speaking, we have seen positive cooperation and collaboration," she said. But she said some problems remained and were the subject of continuing discussions. She said her agency had also requested a meeting with the department to discuss the plan to expand summary deportations — a process known as expedited removal — to the land borders.

Under the new policy, border agents will summarily deport illegal immigrants caught within 100 miles of the Mexican and Canadian borders who have spent up to 14 days within the United States.

Officials said the agents would not focus on deporting Mexicans and Canadians, who will still, for the most part, have their cases heard in immigration court. The agents will concentrate instead on immigrants from other countries. Senior officials said they planned to evaluate the process in Tucson and Laredo before expanding it to other sections of the border.

Safety Stings at Work Sites Will Be Halted

BY STEVEN GREENHOUSE | MARCH 29, 2006

FEDERAL OFFICIALS told immigrant advocates in a letter made public yesterday that government immigration agents would discontinue using undercover sting operations involving health and safety programs to round up illegal immigrants.

Such an operation generated a storm of protest in July when federal agents arrested 48 workers at Seymour Johnson Air Force Base in North Carolina on illegal immigration charges after the agents tricked the workers into attending what was billed as a mandatory training session sponsored by the federal Occupational Safety and Health Administration.

Worker advocates and immigrant groups complained that such activity would discourage immigrant workers from reporting safety violations or seeking help from safety officials at a time when Hispanics were suffering a disproportionately high rate of injuries and fatalities.

On March 17, Marcy M. Forman, director of investigations for the Department of Homeland Security's immigration and customs enforcement division, known as I.C.E., sent a letter to the United Food and Commercial Workers union, which had protested the ruse, to say federal officials were discontinuing the practice.

"This is exactly the action that I.C.E. should have taken," said Jackie Nowell, director of occupational safety for the food and commercial workers union. "Using health and safety as a ruse to catch workers is definitely the wrong way to go when immigrant workers are being killed and injured in far greater numbers than other workers."

Pink Slips at Disney. But First, Training Foreign Replacements.

BY JULIA PRESTON | JUNE 3, 2015

ORLANDO, FLA. — The employees who kept the data systems humming in the vast Walt Disney fantasy fief did not suspect trouble when they were suddenly summoned to meetings with their boss.

While families rode the Seven Dwarfs Mine Train and searched for Nemo on clamobiles in the theme parks, these workers monitored computers in industrial buildings nearby, making sure millions of Walt Disney World ticket sales, store purchases and hotel reservations went through without a hitch. Some were performing so well that they thought they had been called in for bonuses.

Instead, about 250 Disney employees were told in late October that they would be laid off. Many of their jobs were transferred to immigrants on temporary visas for highly skilled technical workers, who were brought in by an outsourcing firm based in India. Over the next three months, some Disney employees were required to train their replacements to do the jobs they had lost.

"I just couldn't believe they could fly people in to sit at our desks and take over our jobs exactly," said one former worker, an American in his 40s who remains unemployed since his last day at Disney on Jan. 30. "It was so humiliating to train somebody else to take over your job. I still can't grasp it."

Disney executives said that the layoffs were part of a reorganization, and that the company opened more positions than it eliminated.

But the layoffs at Disney and at other companies, including the Southern California Edison power utility, are raising new questions about how businesses and outsourcing companies are using the temporary visas, known as H-1B, to place immigrants in technology jobs in the United States. These visas are at the center of a fierce debate in Congress over whether they complement American workers or displace them.

BRIAN BLANCO FOR THE NEW YORK TIMES

The Team Disney building in Lake Buena Vista, Fla., which houses most of the company's technology operations.

According to federal guidelines, the visas are intended for foreigners with advanced science or computer skills to fill discrete positions when American workers with those skills cannot be found. Their use, the guidelines say, should not "adversely affect the wages and working conditions" of Americans. Because of legal loopholes, however, in practice, companies do not have to recruit American workers first or guarantee that Americans will not be displaced.

Too often, critics say, the visas are being used to bring in immigrants to do the work of Americans for less money, with laid-off American workers having to train their replacements.

"The program has created a highly lucrative business model of bringing in cheaper H-1B workers to substitute for Americans," said Ronil Hira, a professor of public policy at Howard University who studies visa programs and has testified before Congress about H-1B visas.

A limited number of the visas, 85,000, are granted each year, and they are in high demand. Technology giants like Microsoft, Facebook and Google repeatedly press for increases in the annual quotas, saying there are not enough Americans with the skills they need.

Many American companies use H-1B visas to bring in small numbers of foreigners for openings demanding specialized skills, according to official reports. But for years, most top recipients of the visas have been outsourcing or consulting firms based in India, or their American subsidiaries, which import workers for large contracts to take over entire in-house technology units — and to cut costs. The immigrants are employees of the outsourcing companies.

In 2013, those firms — including Infosys, Tata Consultancy Services and HCL America, the company hired by Disney — were six of the top 10 companies granted H-1Bs, with each one receiving more than 1,000 visas.

H-1B immigrants work for less than American tech workers, Professor Hira said at a hearing in March of the Senate Judiciary Committee, because of weaknesses in wage regulations. The savings have been 25 percent to 49 percent in recent cases, he told lawmakers.

In a letter in April to top federal authorities in charge of immigration, a bipartisan group of senators called for an investigation of recent "H-1B-driven layoffs," saying, "Their frequency seems to have increased dramatically in the past year alone."

Last year, Southern California Edison began 540 technology layoffs while hiring two Indian outsourcing firms for much of the work. Three Americans who had lost jobs told Senate lawmakers that many of those being laid off had to teach immigrants to perform their functions.

In a statement, the utility said the layoffs were "a difficult business decision," part of a plan "to focus on making significant, strategic changes that can benefit our customers." It noted that some workers hired by the outsourcing firms were Americans.

Fossil, a fashion watchmaker, said it would lay off more than 100 technology employees in Texas this year, transferring the work to

Infosys. The company is planning "knowledge sharing" between the laid-off employees and about 25 new Infosys workers, including immigrants, who will take jobs in Dallas. Fossil is outsourcing tech services "to be more current and nimble" and "reduce costs when possible," it said in a statement.

Among 350 tech workers laid off in 2013 after a merger at Northeast Utilities, an East Coast power company, many had trained H-1B immigrants to do their jobs, several of those workers reported confidentially to lawmakers. They said that as part of their severance packages, they had to sign agreements not to criticize the company publicly.

In Orlando, Disney executives said the reorganization resulting in the layoffs was meant to allow technology operations to focus on producing more innovations. They said that over all, the company had a net gain of 70 tech jobs.

"Disney has created almost 30,000 new jobs in the U.S. over the past decade," said Kim Prunty, a Disney spokeswoman, adding that the company expected its contractors to comply with all immigration laws.

The tech workers laid off were a tiny fraction of Disney's "cast members," as the entertainment conglomerate calls its theme park workers, who number 74,000 in the Orlando area. Employees who lost jobs were allowed a three-month transition with résumé coaching to help them seek other positions in the company, Disney executives said. Of those laid off, 120 took new jobs at Disney, and about 40 retired or left the company before the end of the transition period, while about 90 did not find new Disney jobs, executives said.

Living in a company town, former Disney workers were reluctant to be identified, saying they feared they could jeopardize their chances of finding new jobs with the few other local tech employers. Several workers agreed to interviews, but only on the condition of anonymity.

They said only a handful of those laid off were moved directly by Disney to other company jobs. The rest were left to compete for positions through Disney job websites. Despite the company's figures, few people they knew had been hired, they said, and then often at a lower pay level. No one was offered retraining, they said. One former worker, a 57-year-old man with more than 10 years at Disney, displayed a list of 18 jobs in the company he had applied for. He had not had more than an initial conversation on any one, he said.

Disney "made the difficult decision to eliminate certain positions, including yours," as a result of "the transition of your work to a managed service provider," said a contract presented to employees on the day the layoffs were announced. It offered a "stay bonus" of 10 percent of severance pay if they remained for 90 days. But the bonus was contingent on "the continued satisfactory performance of your job duties." For many, that involved training a replacement. Young immigrants from India took the seats at their computer stations.

"The first 30 days was all capturing what I did," said the American in his 40s, who worked 10 years at Disney. "The next 30 days, they worked side by side with me, and the last 30 days, they took over my job completely." To receive his severance bonus, he said, "I had to make sure they were doing my job correctly."

In late November, this former employee received his annual performance review, which he provided to The New York Times. His supervisor, who was not aware the man was scheduled for layoff, wrote that because of his superior skills and "outstanding" work, he had saved the company thousands of dollars. The supervisor added that he was looking forward to another highly productive year of having the employee on the team.

The employee got a raise. His severance pay had to be recalculated to include it.

The former Disney employee who is 57 worked in project management and software development. His résumé lists a top-level skill certification and command of seven operating systems, 15 program languages and more than two dozen other applications and media.

"I was forced into early retirement," he said. The timing was "horrible," he said, because his wife recently had a medical emergency with expensive bills. Shut out of Disney, he is looking for a new job elsewhere.

Former employees said many immigrants who arrived were younger technicians with limited data skills who did not speak English fluently and had to be instructed in the basics of the work.

HCL America, a branch of a global company based in Noida, India, won a contract with Disney in 2012. In a statement, the company said details of the agreement were confidential. "As a company, we work very closely with the U.S. Department of Labor and strictly adhere to all visa guidelines and requirements to be complied with," it said.

The chairman of the Walt Disney Company, Robert A. Iger, is a co-chairman with Michael R. Bloomberg, the former mayor of New York, and Rupert Murdoch, the executive chairman of News Corporation, in the Partnership for a New American Economy, which pushes for an overhaul of immigration laws, including an increase in H-1B visas.

But Disney directly employs fewer than 10 H-1B workers, executives said, and has not been prominent in visa lobbying. Mr. Iger supports the partnership's broader goals, including increased border security and a pathway to legal status for immigrants here illegally, officials of the organization said.

ICE Deportation Cases: Your Questions Answered

BY NIRAJ CHOKSHI AND VIVIAN YEE | FEB. 13, 2018

THE DETAILS of their immigration cases in widely shared news stories have elicited public sympathy — a 10-year-old stopped on her way to surgery; a mother hiding in a church — but they also raise questions about how the nation's complicated immigration policies are enforced.

Take the cases of Syed Ahmed Jamal and Jesus Berrones, which have received a great deal of national attention in recent weeks. Both men have sympathetic stories, faced deportation and received temporary reprieves.

The treatment of people often seems arbitrary and inconsistent. Mr. Jamal, who was detained and separated from his wife and three children in Kansas, received temporary relief despite the efforts of federal authorities to deport him (which continue), while Mr. Berrones,

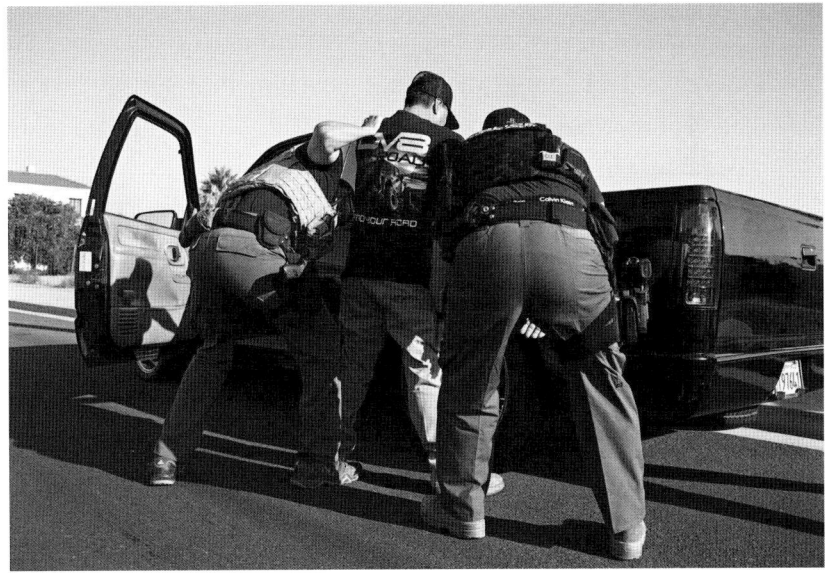

MELISSA LYTTLE FOR THE NEW YORK TIMES

Immigration and Customs Enforcement officers pulling a man over during a traffic stop near his Riverside, Calif., house.

whose 5-year-old son has cancer, was allowed a temporary reprieve on Monday.

The contrast underscores the discretion given to Immigration and Customs Enforcement officials. It also raises questions about the extent of their powers and the rights of detainees. Here are answers to some of those questions.

Q. *Are deportation arrests more common than before?*

A. So far, yes, they are. Between the start of the Trump administration and the end of the 2017 fiscal year, the agency arrested 110,568 people, a 42 percent increase over the same period the year before, according to an ICE report.

Q. *What happens after someone is arrested?*

A. It depends.

If someone in custody already faces an order of deportation, the options may be limited.

Mr. Jamal and nearly one million others fall into this category. In Mr. Jamal's case, an immigration judge gave him until Oct. 26, 2011, to leave the country voluntarily, according to ICE. When he failed to do so, his departure order became a deportation order.

A lawyer may be able to argue, as Mr. Jamal's successfully did, that the judge should temporarily stay the removal. A lawyer may also be able to persuade a judge to reopen a case if a person's circumstances have changed.

But without such a stay, ICE can conclude that the legal process is over and begin deportation as soon as possible, depending on the logistics of sending the individuals to their native country.

That happened to Mr. Jamal on Monday. When his first stay was dissolved, he was placed on a flight. His lawyers said they were able to secure a second stay, however, while his plane was on its way to Hawaii where it would refuel.

An individual in custody without such an order of deportation may have more options — and time.

The detainee can apply for asylum or other such programs. Even if that relief isn't available, immigration courts are often backlogged and arrestees have several rounds of appeals to exhaust, a process that can take some time.

That said, they may have to spend some or all of that time in detention, where many who lack legal representation simply agree to be deported anyway.

Q. *Can ICE make arrests anywhere?*

A. No. There are two kinds of restrictions on the places where immigration officers can make an arrest: legal and self-imposed.

Like other law enforcement agencies, ICE must respect constitutional protections, meaning its officers can't enter a private residence without consent or a warrant, according to Grisel Ruiz, a staff lawyer with the Immigrant Legal Resource Center.

The agency has also vowed on its own to avoid making arrests at "sensitive locations," a policy intended to build trust and allow individuals to engage in some activities "without fear or hesitation."

Those include schools, places of worship, hospitals and public demonstrations. (In response to criticism, ICE recently said it would also put more limits on when it will make arrests in courthouses.)

But that voluntary policy is just that: "It's not binding, it's not law," Ms. Ruiz said.

And she and other immigrant advocates say that while the agency may avoid making arrests at those sensitive locations, it continues to arrest people near them.

Q. *Does ICE have to let deportees get their affairs in order?*

A. While they sometimes do, immigration officers are not required to give arrestees the chance to gather their belongings or even say farewell to their loved ones. Mr. Jamal's family said that the officers who arrested him, for example, denied them the right to hug him goodbye. And, often, those being arrested may be far from home and family.

Depending on the stage of the deportation process and criminal history, some individuals are allowed to go free on the condition that they commit to voluntarily leave the country within a specified period.

Q. *Do contributions to society make any difference?*

A. ICE agents are given discretion to decide whether someone should be deported.

The agency may let someone stay, under supervision, in extenuating circumstances — if the person is receiving medical treatment or caring for an elderly parent, for example. That appears to have been the case for Mr. Berrones, who reportedly received a one-year stay on his removal that will allow him to continue caring for his ill son.

Community pressure, and media attention, has swayed the agency in the past, too.

But, under President Trump, ICE is using that discretion in favor of detainees less often. The administration's position is that anyone who is in the United States illegally is a target for deportation. In the last few years of the Obama administration, on the other hand, agents were told to prioritize some groups, like serious criminals and recent arrivals.

So while family, personal circumstances or contributions to society may be considered, they are less likely to help an individual's cause now than they once were.

Q. *What role does a criminal record, or the lack of one, play?*

A. The Trump administration considers being in the United States without proper documentation to be a crime, a stricter approach than in the past, when immigration offenses were often thought of more like civil infractions.

That means that the agency takes seriously cases in which the only significant mark on someone's record is a failure to comply with a deportation order, as it says was true of Mr. Jamal.

But a lack of a criminal record, apart from immigration offenses, can help to persuade the government to let individuals remain free while they await an administrative decision about their status.

Q. *Do you get points for trying to achieve legal status?*

A. While some immigrants, like asylum seekers, are protected from deportation as they await a decision on their status, merely applying does not provide protection. Without a court order or a government commitment to pause deportation, the only thing that matters is a person's current legal status.

But attempts to achieve legal status can help to persuade a judge that an individual need not be detained, says Jesse Lloyd, an Oakland immigration lawyer who is the vice chairman of the American Immigration Lawyers Association's ICE committee.

"A history of otherwise complying with immigration authorities is at least a good indication that someone's not a flight risk," he said.

Former ICE Lawyer Pleads Guilty to Stealing Immigrants' Identities to Spend $190,000

BY MATTHEW HAAG | FEB. 15, 2018

A FORMER TOP LAWYER for Immigration and Customs Enforcement pleaded guilty on Thursday to stealing the identities of seven people in deportation proceedings and buying more than $190,000 in goods under their names, the federal authorities said.

The former lawyer, Raphael A. Sanchez, used his position as the ICE chief counsel for immigration proceedings in several Western states to gain access to the victims' personal information in federal databases, including their immigration records. Using those records, Mr. Sanchez created fake Social Security cards, driver's licenses and utility bills to open credit card and bank accounts in their names, the authorities said.

MELISSA LYTTLE FOR THE NEW YORK TIMES

An Immigration and Customs Enforcement raid in California in June.

Mr. Sanchez, 44, ran the elaborate scheme, which included his claiming three of the people as dependents on his tax returns, from October 2013 to October 2017, ordering items online and having them shipped to his house. To try to make the purchases appear legitimate, he also signed up for credit monitoring to track the immigrants' credit scores and fabricated income statements, the Justice Department said.

"Raphael Sanchez betrayed that solemn responsibility and abused his official position to prey upon aliens for his own personal gain," John P. Cronan, the acting assistant attorney in the department's criminal division, said in a statement.

Mr. Sanchez pleaded guilty to one count of wire fraud and one count of aggravated identity theft in federal court in Seattle. The charges were filed on Monday in the United States District Court for the Western District of Washington. Mr. Sanchez is scheduled to be sentenced in May.

Mr. Sanchez's lawyer, Cassandra Stamm, said he had "sincere and immense regret" for his actions.

"Raphael Sanchez is a good person who has made serious mistakes in violation of the law," Ms. Stamm said in an email. "Mr. Sanchez looks forward to fully repaying all those affected by his crimes."

As part of his plea agreement, Mr. Sanchez is expected to receive a sentence of 48 months in prison, Ms. Stamm said. Mr. Sanchez resigned from his federal position on Monday.

CHAPTER 2

The Southern Border

Like most countries, the United States receives many immigrants from its direct neighbors. Because of Mexico's comparative poverty, huge numbers of Mexican citizens travel to the United States hoping to build better lives. However, the U.S. government has strict laws about who qualifies to take up residence in the country. Many of those who don't meet the criteria attempt to enter the United States illegally. Unlawful travel across the border can be dangerous. Those who do make it across are not immediately afforded the same rights as documented immigrants — and they risk deportation.

Mexico Fears the Loss of America as a Safety Valve

BY LARRY ROHTER | MARCH 15, 1987

WITH JUST TWO MONTHS remaining before the main provisions of the new United States immigration law go into effect, Mexico is preparing for what many here fear will be a huge influx of returning workers. A tidal wave of reverse migration would strain public services and exacerbate the country's worst economic crisis in 50 years. No one knows exactly what to expect when penalties for employers who knowingly hire illegal aliens take effect June 1. There is "a climate of concern and uncertainty," said the Rev. Florencio Rigoni, secretary of the Roman Catholic Church's Episcopal Commission on Migration.

The questions begin with Mexico's inability to predict how many of its citizens will have to return. Estimates of the number of Mexicans in the United States illegally range upward from 1.5 million. While no reliable figures exist on how many of them will fail to qualify for permanent residency, said Martin Brito Hernandez, the Mexican consul general in Chicago, 200,000 in the Midwest alone could be forced to leave.

The press here, traditionally suspicious of the United States, has raised the specter of large-scale expulsions, adding to the general nervousness. The Government, however, does not appear to take that likelihood seriously. In an interview with the official newspaper El Nacional in December, President Miguel de la Madrid said he thought "the greatest effect of the new law will not be caused by massive deportations of workers to Mexico, at least at levels significantly higher than the present."

What the President and other authorities do anticipate is a significant decrease in the number of people heading northward. United States employers are expected to try to stop hiring people without legal papers. Border surveillance has been tightened and the price of the trip has consequently gone up. Because its population is increasing rapidly, Mexico must create at least one million new jobs a year just to accommodate young workers entering the labor force. And since the start of the economic crisis in 1982, that goal has not been met.

As a result, the importance of the American economy as an escape valve for surplus labor has been growing. Mr. de la Madrid also said that "any reduction in the flow of migration toward the United States can be a serious element in the development of Mexico, since this factor has served as a mechanism of adjustment in regard to employment."

The most immediate effects are expected along the border. Jorge Bustamante, director of the College of the Northern Border in Tijuana, talks of temporary "floating populations" in Mexican border towns, people who will be without jobs, housing and money as they wait for developments on the American side. Already, the Catholic Church reports a doubling of "emergency cases" at its Migrant Assistance Centers in Tijuana, Ciudad Juarez and Matamoros. The church has issued an appeal for financial help on both sides of the border.

Foreign Minister Bernardo Sepulveda Amor has called for the coordination of state and federal authorities to assist "the border states, which may suffer from the phenomenon of re-immigration, with the labor force concentrating itself in the border strip." He announced a task force of officials from the Interior, Budget and Labor and Social Welfare Ministries. But an official said efforts had not advanced beyond "the planning and study stage."

Some here believe that many returning farm workers may go back to their rural homes. Factory workers, however, are expected to head for cities such as Mexico City, Guadalajara and Monterrey where they can use their skills. Both trends are likely to create pressure on housing, transportation and social services. Church leaders have renewed appeals for a program of rural development "so that the countryside can retain its people."

Other anticipated effects include a decrease in the millions of dollars in remittances sent home by workers in the United States. In southern states such as Guerrero and Michoacan, whole villages have come to rely on money from relatives working in the American Southwest. The money was spent in Mexico on construction of new homes, on vehicles and on consumer goods. In addition, many returning workers have complained of "extortion" by Mexican border police who strip them of money or goods after arbitrarily decreeing such items to be "contraband."

Because of the increased risks and costs involved in crossing the border, the type of migrant already seems to be changing. Studies by the College of the Northern Border indicate that those now leaving Mexico have "higher levels of income and skills" than in the past and that the so-called safety valve is turning into a "flight of human capital" at a time when Mexico sorely needs skilled workers to help lift the country out of its deep recession.

No one here, however, believes that the new law and stepped-up patrolling will halt the migratory flow altogether. "There are too many expectations on both sides of the border," Dr. Bustamante of the college said. "On the Mexican side there is the fear of a massive return. On the American side there is the illusion that the new law will put an end to the problem of undocumented workers. Both are exaggerated."

Better Lives for Mexicans Cut Allure of Going North

BY DAMIEN CAVE | JULY 6, 2011

AGUA NEGRA, MEXICO — The extraordinary Mexican migration that delivered millions of illegal immigrants to the United States over the past 30 years has sputtered to a trickle, and research points to a surprising cause: unheralded changes in Mexico that have made staying home more attractive.

A growing body of evidence suggests that a mix of developments — expanding economic and educational opportunities, rising border crime and shrinking families — are suppressing illegal traffic as much as economic slowdowns or immigrant crackdowns in the United States.

Here in the red-earth highlands of Jalisco, one of Mexico's top three states for emigration over the past century, a new dynamic has emerged. For a typical rural family like the Orozcos, heading to El Norte without papers is no longer an inevitable rite of passage. Instead, their homes are filling up with returning relatives; older brothers who once crossed illegally are awaiting visas; and the youngest Orozcos are staying put.

"I'm not going to go to the States because I'm more concerned with my studies," said Angel Orozco, 18. Indeed, at the new technological institute where he is earning a degree in industrial engineering, all the students in a recent class said they were better educated than their parents — and that they planned to stay in Mexico rather than go to the United States.

Douglas S. Massey, co-director of the Mexican Migration Project at Princeton, an extensive, long-term survey in Mexican emigration hubs, said his research showed that interest in heading to the United States for the first time had fallen to its lowest level since at least the 1950s. "No one wants to hear it, but the flow has already stopped," Mr. Massey said, referring to illegal traffic. "For the first time in 60 years, the net traffic has gone to zero and is probably a little bit negative."

The decline in illegal immigration, from a country responsible for roughly 6 of every 10 illegal immigrants in the United States, is stark. The Mexican census recently discovered four million more people in Mexico than had been projected, which officials attributed to a sharp decline in emigration.

American census figures analyzed by the nonpartisan Pew Hispanic Center also show that the illegal Mexican population in the United States has shrunk and that fewer than 100,000 illegal border-crossers and visa-violators from Mexico settled in the United States in 2010, down from about 525,000 annually from 2000 to 2004. Although some advocates for more limited immigration argue that the Pew studies offer estimates that do not include short-term migrants, most experts agree that far fewer illegal immigrants have been arriving in recent years.

The question is why. Experts and American politicians from both parties have generally looked inward, arguing about the success or failure of the buildup of border enforcement and tougher laws limiting illegal immigrants' rights — like those recently passed in Alabama and Arizona. Deportations have reached record highs as total border apprehensions and apprehensions of Mexicans have fallen by more than 70 percent since 2000.

But Mexican immigration has always been defined by both the push (from Mexico) and the pull (of the United States). The decision to leave home involves a comparison, a wrenching cost-benefit analysis, and just as a Mexican baby boom and economic crises kicked off the emigration waves in the 1980s and '90s, research now shows that the easing of demographic and economic pressures is helping keep departures in check.

In simple terms, Mexican families are smaller than they had once been. The pool of likely migrants is shrinking. Despite the dominance of the Roman Catholic Church in Mexico, birth control efforts have pushed down the fertility rate to about 2 children per woman from 6.8 in 1970, according to government figures. So while Mexico added about one million new potential job seekers annually in the 1990s, since 2007 that figure has fallen to an average of 800,000, according to government birth records. By 2030, it is expected to drop to 300,000.

Even in larger families like the Orozcos' — Angel is the 9th of 10 children — the migration calculation has changed. Crossing "mojado," wet or illegally, has become more expensive and more dangerous, particularly with drug cartels dominating the border. At the same time, educational and employment opportunities have greatly expanded in Mexico. Per capita gross domestic product and family income have each jumped more than 45 percent since 2000, according to one prominent economist, Roberto Newell. Despite all the depictions of Mexico as "nearly a failed state," he argued, "the conventional wisdom is wrong."

A significant expansion of legal immigration — aided by American consular officials — is also under way. Congress may be debating immigration reform, but in Mexico, visas without a Congressionally mandated cap on how many people can enter have increased from 2006 to 2010, compared with the previous five years.

State Department figures show that Mexicans who have become American citizens have legally brought in 64 percent more immediate relatives, 220,500 from 2006 through 2010, compared with the figures for the previous five years. Tourist visas are also being granted at higher rates of around 89 percent, up from 67 percent, while American farmers have legally hired 75 percent more temporary workers since 2006.

Edward McKeon, the top American official for consular affairs in Mexico, said he had focused on making legal passage to the United States easier in an effort to prevent people from giving up and going illegally. He has even helped those who were previously illegal overcome bans on entering the United States.

"If people are trying to do the right thing," Mr. McKeon said, "we need to send the signal that we'll reward them."

HARD YEARS IN JALISCO

When Angel Orozco's grandfather considered leaving Mexico in the 1920s, his family said, he wrestled with one elemental question: Will it be worth it?

At that point and for decades to come, yes was the obvious answer. In the 1920s and '30s — when Paul S. Taylor came to Jalisco from California for his landmark study of Mexican emigration — Mexico's central highlands promised little more than hard living. Jobs were scarce and paid poorly. Barely one of three adults could read. Families of 10, 12 and even 20 were common, and most children did not attend school.

Comparatively, the United States looked like a dreamland of technology and riches: Mr. Taylor found that the wages paid by the railroads, where most early migrants found legal work, were five times what could be earned on farms in Arandas, the municipality that includes Agua Negra.

Orozco family members still talk about the benefits of that first trip. Part of the land the extended family occupies today was purchased with American earnings from the 1920s. When Angel's father, Antonio, went north to pick cotton in the 1950s and '60s with the Bracero temporary worker program, which accepted more than 400,000 laborers a year at its peak, working in the United States made even more sense. The difference in wages had reached 10 to 1. Arandas was still dirt poor.

Antonio, with just a few years of schooling, was one of many who felt that with a back as strong as a wooden church door, he could best serve his family from across the border.

"I sent my father money so he could build his house," Antonio said.

Legal status then meant little. After the Bracero program ended in 1964, Antonio said, he crossed back and forth several times without documentation. Passage was cheap. Work lasting for a few months or a year was always plentiful. So when his seven sons started to become adults in the 1990s, he encouraged them to go north as well. Around 2001, he and two of his sons were all in the United States working —

part of what is now recognized as one of the largest immigration waves in American history.

But even then, illegal immigration was becoming less attractive. In the mid-1990s, the Clinton administration added fences and federal agents to what were then the main crossing corridors beyond Tijuana and Ciudad Juárez. The enforcement push, continued by President George W. Bush and President Obama, helped drive up smuggling prices from around $700 in the late 1980s to nearly $2,000 a decade later, and the costs continued to climb, according to research from the Center for Comparative Immigration Studies at the University of California, San Diego. It also shifted traffic to more dangerous desert areas near Arizona.

Antonio said the risks hit home when his nephew Alejandro disappeared in the Sonoran Desert around 2002. A father of one and with a pregnant wife, Alejandro had been promised work by a friend. It took years for the authorities to find his body in the arid brush south of Tucson. Even now, no one knows how he died.

But for the Orozcos, border enforcement was not the major deterrent. Andrés Orozco, 28, a middle son who first crossed illegally in 2000, said that while rising smuggling costs and border crime were worries, there were always ways to avoid American agents. In fact, while the likelihood of apprehension has increased in recent years, 92 to 98 percent of those who try to cross eventually succeed, according to research by Wayne A. Cornelius and his colleagues at the University of California, San Diego.

A PERIOD OF PROGRESS

Another important factor is Mexico itself. Over the past 15 years, this country once defined by poverty and beaches has progressed politically and economically in ways rarely acknowledged by Americans debating immigration. Even far from the coasts or the manufacturing sector at the border, democracy is better established, incomes have generally risen and poverty has declined.

Here in Jalisco, a tequila boom that accelerated through the 1990s created new jobs for farmers cutting agave and for engineers at the stills. Other businesses followed. In 2003, when David Fitzgerald, a migration expert at the University of California, San Diego, came to Arandas, he found that the wage disparity with the United States had narrowed: migrants in the north were collecting 3.7 times what they could earn at home.

That gap has recently shrunk again. The recession cut into immigrant earnings in the United States, according to the Pew Hispanic Center, even as wages have risen in Mexico, according to World Bank figures. Jalisco's quality of life has improved in other ways, too. About a decade ago, the cluster of the Orozco ranches on Agua Negra's outskirts received electricity and running water. New census data shows a broad expansion of such services: water and trash collection, once unheard of outside cities, are now available to more than 90 percent of Jalisco's homes. Dirt floors can now be found in only 3 percent of the state's houses, down from 12 percent in 1990.

Still, education represents the most meaningful change. The census shows that throughout Jalisco, the number of senior high schools or preparatory schools for students aged 15 to 18 increased to 724 in 2009, from 360 in 2000, far outpacing population growth. The Technological Institute of Arandas, where Angel studies engineering, is now one of 13 science campuses created in Jalisco since 2000 — a major reason professionals in the state, with a bachelor's degree or higher, also more than doubled to 821,983 in 2010, up from 405,415 in 2000.

Similar changes have occurred elsewhere. In the poor southern states of Chiapas and Oaxaca, for instance, professional degree holders rose to 525,874 from 244,322 in 2000.

And the data from secondary schools like the one the Orozcos attended in Agua Negra suggests that the trend will continue. Thanks to a Mexican government program called "schools of quality" the campus of three buildings painted sunflower yellow has five new computers for its 71 students, along with new books.

Teachers here, in classrooms surrounded by blue agave fields, say that enrollment is down slightly because families are having fewer children, and instead of sending workers north, some families have moved to other Mexican cities — a trend also found in academic field research. Around half the students now move on to higher schooling, up from 30 percent a decade ago.

"They're identifying more with Mexico," said Agustín Martínez González, a teacher. "With more education, they're more likely to accept reality here and try to make it better."

Some experts agree. Though Mexicans with Ph.D.'s tend to leave for bigger paychecks abroad, "if you have a college degree you're much more likely to stay in Mexico because that is surely more valuable in Mexico," said Jeffrey S. Passel, a demographer at the Pew Hispanic Center.

If these trends — particularly Mexican economic growth — continue over the next decade, Mr. Passel said, changes in the migration dynamic may become even clearer. "At the point where the U.S. needs the workers again," he said, "there will be fewer of them."

PRAYING FOR PAPERS

The United States, of course, has not lost its magnetic appeal. Illegal traffic from Central America has not dropped as fast as it has from Mexico, and even in Jalisco town plazas are now hangouts for men in their 30s with tattoos, oversize baseball caps and a desire to work again in California or another state. Bars with American names — several have adopted Shrek — signal a back and forth that may never disappear.

But more Mexicans are now traveling legally. Several Orozco cousins have received temporary worker visas in the past few years. In March, peak migration season for Jalisco, there were 15 people from Agua Negra at the border waiting to cross.

"And 10 had visas," said Ramón Orozco, 30, another son of Antonio who works in the town's government office after being the first in his family to go to college. "A few years ago there would have been 100, barely any with proper documents."

This is not unique to Agua Negra. A few towns away at the hillside shrine of St. Toribio, the patron saint of migrants, prayers no longer focus on asking God to help sons, husbands or brothers crossing the desert. "Now people are praying for papers," said María Guadalupe, 47, a longtime volunteer.

How did this happen?

Partly, emigrants say, illegal life in the United States became harder. Laws restricting illegal immigrants' rights or making it tougher for employers to hire them have passed in more than a dozen states since 2006. The same word-of-mouth networks that used to draw people north are now advising against the journey. "Without papers all you're thinking about is, when are the police going to stop you or what other risks are you going to face," said Andrés Orozco.

Andrés, a horse lover who drives a teal pickup from Texas, is one of many Orozcos now pinning their hopes on a visa. And for the first time in years, the chances have improved.

Mexican government estimates based on survey data show not just a decrease in migration overall, but also an increase in border crossings with documents. In 2009, the most recent year for which data is available, 38 percent of the total attempted crossings, legal and illegal, were made with documents. In 2007, only 20 percent involved such paperwork.

The Mexican data counts attempted crossings, not people, and does not differentiate between categories of visas. Nor does it mention how long people stayed, nor whether all the documents were valid.

Advocates of limited immigration worry that the issuing of more visas creates a loophole that can be abused. Between 40 and 50 percent of the illegal immigrants in the United States entered legally with visas they overstayed, as of 2005, according to the Pew Hispanic Center.

More recent American population data, however, shows no overall increase in the illegal Mexican population. That suggests that most of legal immigration, say it still may not be enough in a country where the baby boomers are retiring in droves.

Farmers still complain that the H-2A visa program is too complicated and addresses only a portion of the total demand. As of 2010, there were 1,381,896 Mexicans still waiting for their green-card applications to be accepted or rejected. And the United States currently makes only 5,000 green cards annually available worldwide for low-wage workers to immigrate permanently; in recent years, only a few of those have gone to Mexicans.

On the other side, Steven A. Camarota, a demographer at the Center for Immigration Studies in Washington, which favors reduced immigration, said that increasing the proportion of legal entries did little good.

"If you believe there is significant job competition at the bottom end of the labor market, as I do, you're not fixing the problem," Mr. Camarota said. "If you are concerned about the fiscal cost of unskilled immigration and everyone comes in on temporary visas and overstays, or even if they don't, the same problems are likely to apply."

By his calculations, unskilled immigrants like the Orozcos have, over the years, helped push down hourly wages, especially for young, unskilled American workers. Immigrants are also more likely to rely on welfare, he said, adding to public costs.

The Orozco clan, however, may point to a different future. Angel Orozco, like many other young Mexicans, now talks about the United States not as a place to earn money, but rather as a destination for fun and spending.

Today he is just a lanky, shy freshman wearing a Daughtry T-shirt and living in a two-room apartment with only a Mexican flag and a rosary for decoration.

But his dreams are big and local. After graduating, he said, he hopes to work for a manufacturing company in Arandas, which seems likely because the director of his school says that nearly 90 percent of graduates find jobs in their field. Then, Angel said, he will be able to buy what he really wants: a shiny, new red Camaro.

Immigration; A Tale of Two Elections

BY JULIÁN AGUILAR | JAN. 1, 2012

RELATIONS ALONG the Texas-Mexico border depend on the outcome of two elections, one at home and one abroad.

Some posit that if President Obama is re-elected, he may finally act on his 2008 campaign promise to fix the country's immigration system. He has called for this for years, but has simultaneously deported more illegal immigrants than any other president. Between Attorney General Eric H. Holder Jr.'s recent visit to Texas and the United States Justice Department's crackdown on enforcement of Arizona's controversial immigration law — which Texas lawmakers continue to toy with — his administration appears to be working to counteract this reputation.

If a Republican wins the White House, will that president embrace more extreme measures on the border, including a more extensive fence, an infusion of American troops or intervention by the United States in the sovereign nation of Mexico?

Meanwhile, officials on both sides of the border think Mexico's fight against organized drug crime could hinge on that country's presidential election. President Felipe Calderón of the PAN party, cannot run again in next summer's election, and his party has yet to determine who will vie for the seat.

The PRI, the opposition party that held power for 70 years, will most likely field the former governor of the state of Mexico, Enrique Peña Nieto, who has said he does not believe the military is the best tool to fight organized crime — there have been more than 42,000 murders nationwide in drug-related violence since late 2006.

The leftist PRD could run Andrés Manuel López Obrador, who lost to Mr. Calderón 2006 in the country's closest presidential election in history.

American Children, Now Struggling to Adjust to Life in Mexico

BY DAMIEN CAVE | JUNE 18, 2012

IZÚCAR DE MATAMOROS, MEXICO — Jeffrey Isidoro sat near the door of his fifth-grade classroom here in central Mexico, staring outside through designer glasses that, like his Nike sneakers and Nike backpack, signaled a life lived almost entirely in the United States. His parents are at home in Mexico. Jeffrey is lost.

When his teacher asked in Spanish how dolphins communicate, a boy next to him reached over to underline the right answer. When it was Jeffrey's turn to read, his classmates laughed and shouted "en inglés, en inglés" — causing Jeffrey to blush.

"Houston is home," Jeffrey said during recess, in English. "The houses and stuff here, it's all a little strange. I feel, like, uncomfortable."

Never before has Mexico seen so many American Jeffreys, Jennifers and Aidens in its classrooms. The wave of deportations in the past few years, along with tougher state laws and persistent unemployment, have all created a mass exodus of Mexican parents who are leaving with their American sons and daughters.

In all, 1.4 million Mexicans — including about 300,000 children born in the United States — moved to Mexico between 2005 and 2010, according to Mexican census figures. That is roughly double the rate of southbound migration from 1995 to 2000, and new government data published this month suggest that the flow is not diminishing. The result is an entire generation of children who blur the line between Mexican and American.

"It's really a new phenomenon," said Víctor Zúñiga, a sociologist at the University of Monterrey, in Nuevo León State, which borders Texas. "It's the first time in the relationship between Mexico and the United States that we have a generation of young people sharing both societies during the early years of their lives."

SHAUL SCHWARZ FOR THE NEW YORK TIMES

Jeffrey Isidoro, 10, misses Houston and has had a hard time making friends at school in Izúcar de Matamoros in central Mexico.

Critics of immigration have mostly welcomed the mass departure, but demographers and educators worry that far too many American children are being sent to schools in Mexico that are not equipped to integrate them. And because research shows that most of these children plan to return to the United States, some argue that what is Mexico's challenge today will be an American problem tomorrow, with a new class of emerging immigrants: young adults with limited skills, troubled childhoods and the full rights of American citizenship.

"These kinds of changes are really traumatic for kids," said Marta Tienda, a sociologist at Princeton who was born in Texas to Mexican migrant laborers. "It's going to stick with them."

Jeffrey's situation is increasingly common. His father, Tomás Isidoro, 39, a carpenter, was one of the 46,486 immigrants deported in the first half of 2011 who said they had American children, according to a report by Immigration and Customs Enforcement to Congress. That is eight times the half-year average for such removals from 1998 to 2007.

Mr. Isidoro, wearing a Dallas Cowboys hat in his parents' kitchen, said he was still angry that his 25 years of work in the United States meant nothing; that being caught with a broken taillight on his vehicle and without immigration papers meant more than having two American sons — Jeffrey, 10, and his brother, Tommy Jefferson, 2, who was named after the family's favorite president.

As for President Obama, Mr. Isidoro uttered an expletive. "There are all these drug addicts, drug dealers, people who do nothing in the United States, and you're going to kick people like me out," he said. "Why?"

White House officials have said that under a new policy focused on criminals, fewer parents of American children are being deported for minor offenses. On Friday, the Obama administration also announced that hundreds of thousands of illegal immigrants who came to United States as children would be allowed to stay without fear of deportation. The policy, however, does not grant legal status, and because nearly half of the country's 10.2 million illegal immigrant adults have children, experts say that inevitably more families will be divided — especially if deportations over all hold steady around 400,000 a year.

But for Jeffrey, the impact of his father's removal in June last year was immediate. His grades dipped. His mother, Leivi Rodríguez, 32, worried that he had become more distant, from both his friends and his studies. Almost every day, Jeffrey told her he wanted to see his father.

So six months after her husband's deportation, she sent Jeffrey to live with his father in Mexico, and she followed with Tommy a few months later. It was December when he arrived here in a hill town south of Mexico City, surrounded by fields of swaying sugar cane. On Jeffrey's first night, he noticed something strange in his bed. "Dad, what's that?" he asked.

"A scorpion," his father said.

School here presented new challenges, as well. Jeffrey went hungry at first because neither he nor his father realized that without a

SHAUL SCHWARZ FOR THE NEW YORK TIMES

Tomás Isidoro, Jeffrey's father, was deported after living 25 years in the United States.

cafeteria, students relied on their parents to bring them food at recess.

In class, Jeffrey's level of confusion rises and falls. His teacher said she struggled to keep him from daydreaming. "His body is here, but his mind — who knows where it is," she said.

Houston — that is where Jeffrey's thoughts typically drift. There, he had friends, McDonald's, the zoo. It is where he lingered at the library at Gleason Elementary to catch up on his favorite series of books, "Diary of a Wimpy Kid." There, his school had a playground; here, there is just a concrete slab. There, computers were common; here, there are none.

"It was just better," Jeffrey said.

The educational disparities between Mexico and the United States are not always so stark. At the elementary level, some of Mexico's schools are on par with, or even stronger than, the overcrowded, underfinanced American schools that serve many immigrant children, education experts say.

DIGITAL LIGHT SOURCE/UIG VIA GETTY IMAGES

Students work on assignments in their classroom in Ciudad Juárez. The largest city in the Mexican state of Chihuahua, Ciudad Juárez is just south of El Paso, Texas.

But Mexican schools lag when it comes to secondary education. In many areas of Mexico, especially places where the tradition of migration is not as well established, Mexico's educational bureaucracy can make life difficult for new arrivals like Jeffrey. It is not uncommon for American students to be barred from enrollment for a year or more because they lack proper documents.

"The established rules for registration don't need to be so severe," said Armando Reynoso Carrillo, a state legislator from Malinalco, a rural area in Mexico State where dozens of American children have arrived in recent years.

The problems extend beyond registration. Mexicans have a long history of greeting returnees with skepticism — for abandoning Mexico, or because they resent the United States, or view those who moved there as materialistic, culturally out of touch and arrogant. The prejudice often extends to their children.

Graciela Treviño González said that when she returned to Malinalco three years ago, after more than a decade in California, she could not get her American son onto a soccer team because the coaches refused to accept him without Mexican identification. "He felt rejected by everyone," she said. "The kids called him 'leche,' 'gringo' — it was awful." Leche means milk and gringo can range from a neutral reference to a foreigner to a slur.

Here in the central state of Puebla, Mexican children are especially likely to see transnational students as different, according to surveys by Mr. Zúñiga, the sociologist. Some have come to Mexico because of deportations. Others arrived because relatives were sick or without work.

But regardless of the cause, Mexican students tend to see their American-educated colleagues as strangers. Jeffrey's experience is typical: He is friendly and quick to open up in English, but quieter at school, where Spanish is the only language one hears.

At one point this spring, as Jeffrey sat at the edge of the playground, a larger boy approached from behind and asked if he was from Florida or Houston. When Jeffrey pulled away because the boy had leaned into him, the bigger boy seemed surprised. "Are you mad?" he asked.

Later, other boys tested Jeffrey on his English, asking him in Spanish to translate various body parts.

"How do you say foot?" one asked. "Finger?"

"Eye?"

Jeffrey provided one-word answers without enthusiasm. At home, a three-room concrete box with furniture hauled from Houston, he said that many of the children called him Four Eyes. He said he was starting to feel more comfortable academically and socially, but even in a school with 11 other children born or educated in the United States (out of 296) he is still a foreigner. Sometimes, he confuses the Mexican pledge of allegiance with the American version.

Ms. Tienda, at Princeton, said children of Jeffrey's age were more likely to struggle with such a difficult transition. "This is the age where they start to be aware of each other's differences," she said. "They're preadolescents and their identity is being crystallized."

She added that how these students fared over the long term will probably vary widely. Some will make the transition easily while others will suffer setback after setback. It will depend on their language skills, school and family dynamics.

Jeffrey, like many other children whose parents have moved them to a country they do not know, seems to be teetering between catching up to his classmates and falling further behind. His parents are struggling to find work and keep their marriage together. Jeffrey, in quieter moments, said he was just trying to endure until he could go home.

"I dream, like, I'm sleeping in the United States," he said. "But when I wake up, I'm in Mexico."

How One Sport Is Keeping a Language, and a Culture, Alive

BY WALTER THOMPSON-HERNÁNDEZ | MARCH 13, 2018

THE MEN GATHER at an open field in a recreation area of the San Fernando Valley every Sunday, putting chalk to the dusty ground to draw the boundaries of a game that has been a weekly ritual as long as many can remember. After they are done, these men and others who filter in cluster into distinct teams, tossing a six-pound rubber ball to warm up.

On a recent Sunday, one of them, Jorge Cruz, 39, lifted a 15-pound glove studded with nails and other ornamentation in the air. He glanced back at his teammates and asked, "You guys ready?" in Zapotec, an indigenous Oaxacan language, before bouncing the ball on a cement slab known as el saque and hitting it toward the opposing team.

G L ASKEW II FOR THE NEW YORK TIMES

At first glance, pelota mixteca might resemble elements of baseball, volleyball and tennis, but a closer examination reveals a bit more nuance. Each jugada, or game, involves approximately 10 players, and begins when one player initiates a serve from the cement slab.

This is how you start a game of pelota mixteca, a ballgame said by its players in California to have originated hundreds of years ago in Oaxaca, Mexico, though theories abound about whether it is an offshoot of an ancient Mesoamerican game or a European sport brought to the New World. Wherever it arrived, it serves not only as a pastime: It is also a way of keeping its players' culture alive, and serves as a network for an immigrant community throughout the West Coast. It has even spawned an under-the-radar international tournament.

"My dad first brought me out here when I was 17, but now I come on my own and I bring my children," Jorge Cruz said, pausing during one of the games. "He would always tell me that this was one of the ways that we could preserve our culture."

He is not alone. More than two dozen other Oaxacan players who speak indigenous languages like Zapotec and Mixtec travel to the pasajuegos (games) every week from Southern and Northern California cities, and each makes the journey to the San Fernando Valley for many of the same reasons.

Mr. Cruz's father, Reynaldo Cruz, 71, introduced the game to his son to preserve Oaxacan culture and his family's native language. The elder Cruz speaks an Oaxacan language known as Valle (valley), as well as Zapotec, an indigenous language spoken by 400,000 people, which is recognized more frequently, according to Pamela Munro, a professor of linguistics at the University of California, Los Angeles.

Because a majority of the pelota mixteca players live in communities where Spanish or English are spoken rather than Zapotec, second-generation Oaxacan children are less likely to preserve that language or any of the other indigenous languages spoken during play.

"They often shy away from speaking their indigenous language because of the legacy of racism, which forces them to sometimes hide and cloak their identities," said Rafael Vásquez, 37, a scholar who is working on a book about Mexican ethnicity and multilingualism.

G L ASKEW II FOR THE NEW YORK TIMES

Jorge Cruz, 39.

"When there's a safe space they often feel more free to speak in their native languages."

Most of the men who play pelota mixteca are first-generation immigrants who were part of successive waves of Oaxacans who settled in and around Los Angeles beginning in the 1980s. Like Reynaldo Cruz, many of these people chose to live in Oaxacan communities.

For second-generation Oaxacan youths in the United States, speaking indigenous languages in school or public spaces is often met with sharp ridicule because of negative stereotypes from Mexican-Americans, the scholars said.

"Many Spanish speakers in Mexico are quite prejudiced against people who speak indigenous languages," Ms. Munro said. "The Spanish term indio (Indian) in Mexico is a highly prejudicial term, and a lot of that carries over to indigenous people in the U.S."

At the same time, some families believe that learning Spanish instead of their indigenous language provides more economic opportunities both in the U.S. and in Mexico, according to Mr. Vasquez.

A number of Oaxacan youths are making efforts to "revitalize" these indigenous languages by playing sports like pelota mixteca and making frequent trips to Oaxaca. It provides an environment free from the stigma or the expectation to adopt Spanish.

Still, pelota mixteca is far from a perfect game. And while most of the men are married and are doting husbands and fathers, the game reveals strong questions about the role of gender in the sport. Women are not on the field and if the men's wives attend the games, they often look after the children while their husbands play.

Some of the players believe that women cannot handle the physical strain of the game, said Paula Mota, 25, a graduate student at California State University, Northridge, who has spent three years observing and researching this group of pelota mixteca players. But she added that there were some women's teams in Mexico.

What began as a game between local Los Angeles residents almost 20 years ago has in recent years emerged as an under-the-radar

A glove and balls used in pelota mixteca. Players must order their gloves from highly sought-out artisans who live in Oaxaca, a process that can take up to a few months and cost between $200 and $300.

international tournament, with players coming from as far as Texas and Oaxaca twice a year to play in local tournaments.

Other players — particularly those who are undocumented — use the pelota mixteca social media network as a way to share helpful information for community members facing the threat of deportation, particularly when traveling to and from tournaments.

News about laws like SB-1070, a bill that passed in Arizona in 2010 that requires the police to determine the immigration status of people detained or arrested when there is "reasonable suspicion" of their immigration status, spread throughout the pelota mixteca community and caused concern among players who hoped to travel to different states to play. At the same time, the widespread accessibility of social media has meant that it is a place where players can strategize about safe travel routes.

Pelota mixteca continues to be played in relative obscurity every

Sunday, but a younger generation of players has appeared on the field. Mr. Cruz now brings his son Jorge, 15, and his nephew, Miguel Angel, 9, to the games with him every weekend, as his father once did more than 20 years ago.

The rally ended and the younger Jorge Cruz, walked off the field to take a break from the blazing San Fernando Valley heat. "I feel empowered and excited that I'm playing the same game that my ancestors did," he said while catching his breath. "If I have children one day, I'm going to teach them this game, too, so that they don't lose our heritage."

Texas Banned 'Sanctuary Cities.' Some Police Departments Didn't Get the Memo.

BY MANNY FERNANDEZ | MARCH 15, 2018

HOUSTON — It is often called Texas' "show me your papers" law, but few papers are actually being shown in some of the state's biggest cities.

A federal appeals court on Tuesday largely upheld the Texas immigration law known as Senate Bill 4, which bans so-called sanctuary cities in the state. Among other provisions, the bill allows police officers to question the immigration status of anyone they arrest or detain, including during routine traffic stops.

But months after portions of the law went into effect in September, prompting legal battles and fierce debates about whether it could lead to widespread racial profiling, officers in some Texas cities appear to be asking about immigration status only in very rare cases. And even after the court's ruling this week, officials in those cities are not planning to make them change.

"From an operational standpoint, from a policy standpoint, it will have no impact," Chief Art Acevedo of the Houston Police Department said of the law. "The problem is the perception problem that it creates, that local police officers are going to be more interested in immigration enforcement of people who don't bother anybody."

Here in Houston, the state's most populous city, the police department said officers had asked detainees about their immigration status only twice since September. In Austin, city officials said it had happened just once. All of the officer inquiries were reviewed by officials, who said that they were relevant to investigations and did not amount to racial profiling.

"We have a code for it so we can track it," said Chief Acevedo, who requires his officers to document all immigration-status interactions.

"When we reviewed the data two weeks ago, out of tens of thousands of contacts this department has had, we've had two inquiries."

Senate Bill 4, or S.B. 4, does not require all officers to ask about a person's immigration status, but instead allows them to ask those questions at the officers' discretion.

The low number of reported inquiries illustrates the conflict between the state Republican leaders behind the law and local elected officials and law enforcement in largely Democratic major cities like Austin, Dallas, Houston and San Antonio.

Officials in those cities, several of which have sued Texas seeking to overturn the law, are trying to walk a fine line between complying with the measure and minimizing its impact on their operations. They have followed requests from immigration authorities to hold detainees suspected of being in the country illegally — another provision in S.B. 4 — while reassuring anxious and outraged immigrants in their communities.

After the ruling on Tuesday, the mayor of Houston, Sylvester Turner, made an unscheduled appearance at a rally by opponents of the law outside City Hall. "It remains my position that the Houston Police Department is not U.S. Immigration and Customs Enforcement and H.P.D. should not function as an arm of ICE," Mr. Turner said later in a statement.

State leaders were unwavering. "Hopefully this ruling will make the law crystal clear for those liberal public officials in some Texas cities who have flaunted their opposition to S.B. 4 and misrepresented its intent," Lt. Gov. Dan Patrick, a Republican, said in a statement.

Supporters of the law viewed the ruling as a victory, including conservative leaders in other states seeking to pass similar bans on sanctuary cities, jurisdictions that limit cooperation between local law enforcement and federal immigration authorities.

Republican lawmakers in Florida tried but failed to pass a bill banning sanctuary cities this legislative session. But the Republican speaker of the Florida House, Richard Corcoran, who has pushed for a crackdown, said the ruling on Tuesday in the Texas case would help their cause.

"The linchpin of the sanctuary defenders' argument was that courts would find such legislation unconstitutional," Mr. Corcoran said in a statement. "We knew they were wrong, and today the court agreed. Any elected official who thinks they can choose which laws they will and will not follow is sadly mistaken and this ruling reinforces that fundamental American truth."

In addition to prohibiting sanctuary policies, S.B. 4 threatens officials who violate the law with fines, jail time and removal from office. The measure was backed by the state's Republican governor and lieutenant governor, and passed by the Republican-controlled Legislature.

Austin, Dallas, Houston and other cities and counties sued Texas to block the law, saying it was unconstitutional, opened the door to racial profiling and would make documented and undocumented immigrants fearful of reporting crimes and cooperating with the police.

The ruling on Tuesday by a three-judge panel of the United States Court of Appeals for the Fifth Circuit only complicates the situation. Parts of the law went into effect after a court ruling in September. The Fifth Circuit opinion allows nearly all of the law's provisions to kick in, although lawyers for the localities and groups suing the state said they were considering appealing the decision to either the full Fifth Circuit or the Supreme Court.

Despite upholding most of the law's provisions, the Fifth Circuit's decision could narrow the effect of the law. The ruling suggested that local officials who limit their cooperation with federal immigration enforcement because of limited resources were not necessarily violating the law.

"It is not 100 percent obvious what is allowed and not allowed as far as policymaking," said Thomas A. Saenz, the president and general counsel of the Mexican American Legal Defense and Educational Fund, which represents San Antonio and other jurisdictions and groups in the lawsuit. "You don't know how it's going to be put into effect in the field."

The Fifth Circuit judges struck down one provision of the law — a clause that had barred officials even from endorsing policies that limit immigration enforcement, which the judges said violated the First Amendment. But some local leaders are concerned that the free speech rights of city employees remain restricted by the law, because the judges lifted the endorsement prohibition only for elected officials and not for nonelected government personnel.

On Wednesday in San Antonio, some of those dynamics seemed to be at play. Shortly before the start of a news conference held by groups opposed to the law, Councilman Rey Saldaña wondered whether the city's police chief, William McManus, would speak at the event. Mr. Saldaña invited Chief McManus — who is an appointed official, not an elected one — but the chief did not attend.

"I'm protected according to the Fifth Circuit, because I'm an elected official, but the police chief is not," Mr. Saldaña said. "He works for the city. It gets us to the point where we might just have to wear a muzzle around our face with respect to whether we can truly represent the interests of community members that come to us."

CHAPTER 3

Children and Dreamers

Children born within the United States are automatically granted citizenship even if their immigrant parents may not be able to legally remain in the country. However, children born outside of the United States and brought in by their parents are not guaranteed citizenship or even residency, and they may be undocumented immigrants without even knowing it. These children can face lifelong legal struggles to remain in the only place they have ever lived.

I.N.S. Ruling Benefits Illegal Immigrant Children

BY MARVINE HOWE | MARCH 26, 1988

UNDOCUMENTED IMMIGRANT CHILDREN who are or have been in foster care will no longer be disqualified from becoming legal residents of the United States, according to a modification of immigration policy.

In a policy reversal, the Immigration and Naturalization Service has ruled that cash assistance to foster parents will no longer be considered as public cash assistance, which would have disqualified foster children for legalization under the Immigration Reform and Control Act of 1987.

The revision, dated March 23 and signed by the immigration agency's associate commissioner, Richard E. Norton, follows a Federal suit to protect the right of children under foster care to become legal residents. The suit, in which New York City and the Legal Aid Society joined, was filed earlier this month.

"It's a terrific victory for Peter Zimroth and the children of New York," Mayor Koch said, referring to the city's Corporation Counsel. The Mayor had called the original policy "another example of the Federal Government's mean-spirited approach to the needs of the most helpless members of our society."

Mr. Zimroth added: "The I.N.S. did the right thing, in the spirit of Congressional intent for the amnesty program."

Under the immigration act, undocumented aliens were given one year, ending May 4, to apply for legal status. To be eligible for legalization, aliens must prove continuous residence in the United States since Jan. 1, 1982, and demonstrate that they are "not likely to become a financial charge."

REVIEW OF ENTIRE ISSUE

In its policy memorandum, the I.N.S. declared that, as a result of many inquiries on the eligibility of foster children for legalization, the agency had reviewed the entire foster care issue and concluded that children in such programs would "not be considered to have received public cash assistance."

In summary, the memorandum stated: "Due to the fact that no monetary payment is made to the child or the child's family in a foster care environment and that the benefit received by the child from the program is a result of judicial order, the services received should be considered in-kind assistance."

Lynne Kelly, a Legal Aid lawyer, expressed delight with the immigration service's decision, saying it applied nationwide. An estimated 1,000 undocumented immigrant children are in foster care.

In New York City, the Human Resources Administration's Special Services for Children has already identified 30 to 40 foster care children who should qualify for amnesty immediately, according to Elissa Hutner, the deputy general counsel for the department.

Legal Aid estimates that the service's action could affect 100 to 300 children who are in New York State's foster care system or have gone through it.

Mixed Scorecard for Immigrants' Children

BY FORD FESSENDEN | OCT. 21, 2007

A NEW JERSEY child welfare group concluded in its first report on children in immigrant families last week that most are English-speaking and American-born but at a competitive disadvantage in school because their parents are working harder, making less and struggling with English.

Nearly one in three children in the state comes from a family with at least one immigrant member, the report from the Association for Children of New Jersey said, and they will be a substantial part of the state's future economic prospects.

The group's findings come as Asian and Hispanic students are swelling suburban schools: Statewide, their numbers have risen to more than one million, up from 840,000 in 2000, according to state figures.

The report is an attempt to put children on the agenda of Gov. Jon S. Corzine's Blue Ribbon Advisory Panel on Immigrant Policy, a 15-member task force appointed in August to figure out how to make sure immigrants are not marginalized, said Cecilia Zalkind, executive director of the nonprofit association. "As we look at what New Jersey has to do to prepare our future workforce, these kids will be a big part of that," said Ms. Zalkind, whose group regularly issues reports on the welfare of children in the state but has never focused on immigrant children before. "Their opportunities for success will to a great degree determine the state's prosperity."

Along with California and New York, New Jersey has become a leading immigrant gateway. With 1.6 million immigrants, it ranks third in the proportion of its population, 20 percent, that is foreign born. There were 646,000 children in New Jersey families with at least one immigrant member in 2005, up from 552,000 in 2000.

Using census data, the group concluded that children in immigrant families are better off economically in New Jersey (with median income of $65,400) than in most of the rest of the country ($46,500 nationwide).

But though they are more likely to have at least one parent working than native-born families in the state, immigrant families make substantially less money, according to the report; the native-born families have a median income of $78,700.

The immigrant families are also less likely to have medical insurance. About 59 percent own their own homes, far below the 74 percent of native-born families.

While the number of children with limited English ability is low, the report says, the language ability of their parents is another matter. One in five immigrant children lives in a home in which no adult speaks English well, the report says. Children with working parents who do not speak English well are less likely to get academic support at home and thus are "at a significant disadvantage compared to families with English-speaking adults," the report says.

The report mostly treats immigrants as a monolithic group, but it points out that they come from widely different ethnic and economic backgrounds. For instance, immigrants are both more likely to have a college degree and more likely to lack even a high school degree when compared with native-born residents.

That is because the immigrant wave is split, with many educated workers in the region's technology and financial-services industries, and many unskilled laborers in the landscaping, construction and restaurant industries.

But what most children in immigrant families have in common, Ms. Zalkind said, is that they are Americans, even if their parents are not.

"A surprising statistic to us is that 87 percent of the children are citizens," she said, "and that suggests they're here and part of the United States, and will be part of New Jersey in the future."

For DACA Recipients, Losing Protection and Work Permits Is Just the Start

BY CAITLIN DICKERSON | SEPT. 7, 2017

IT IS NOT JUST the threat of deportation that is hanging over Amparo Gonzalez. The 31-year-old single mother could also lose her job at a warehouse company, even if she stays in the country. With it would go the health insurance she gets through her employer, which covers her 13-year-old daughter, as well as the exams and treatments that Ms. Gonzalez needs for her chronic colon disease.

"I lose everything without DACA," she said, referring to the Deferred Action for Childhood Arrivals program that President Trump moved this week to eliminate.

With the news that roughly 800,000 people across the country would begin losing their protected status under DACA, which offered work permits and temporary reprieves from deportation to young undocumented immigrants, the program's beneficiaries are now scrambling to prepare for the various ways the decision could upend their lives.

Living and working in the United States are the two privileges most often associated with DACA. But for many recipients, those are merely the first dominoes to fall if Congress does not pass a replacement. The shutdown of the program could reverberate far beyond those privileges and topple the many others that DACA protection can confer, from state-sponsored health coverage and financial aid to driver's licenses and professional credentials. The loss of these things could, in turn, disrupt recipients' abilities to go to school, support their families and keep a roof over their heads.

Losing the ability to work legally would mean, for an estimated 450,000 people, forfeiting the health insurance and other benefits offered through employers, according to the National Immigration

Law Center. Another 290,000 recipients, the center said, may lose their eligibility for state-subsidized health coverage when their protection expires.

The law center's researchers also found that more than half of DACA beneficiaries will be forced to relinquish driver's licenses. And while many might find work under the table or from sympathetic employers, they could not obtain most occupational licenses, like those required for nursing and cosmetology.

Although DACA's deportation protections lasted only two years before needing to be renewed, widespread bipartisan support gave many recipients the confidence to make risky life decisions such as buying homes, pursuing graduate degrees and starting families. Those decisions came with major obligations that may be unmanageable without a steady job or benefits, but that cannot be canceled or renegotiated.

ALEX WROBLEWSKI FOR THE NEW YORK TIMES

Protesters demonstrated in support of recipients of the Deferred Action for Childhood Arrivals program in Washington in 2017.

"It's just incalculable," Thomas A. Saenz, president and general counsel of the Mexican American Legal Defense and Educational Fund said. "Any of the things that DACA provides are things that we all take for granted and cannot even imagine living without."

The extent of the impact will depend largely on where recipients live. DACA beneficiaries were never eligible for federal health care programs like Medicaid or Medicare, nor for federal student loans; many of the rights and privileges they enjoyed are regulated at the state level. Some state governments may pass new laws or interpret existing law in ways that allow benefits to continue; others may not.

If state efforts in New York and California are unsuccessful, a combined 265,000 DACA recipients in those states will retain access to in-state college tuition, but may lose access to state-subsidized health care benefits.

In New York, they would no longer be eligible for state-funded grants and student loans, and would no longer be able to drive legally. That may have a limited impact on immigrants in transit-rich New York City, but could be debilitating for those who work on farms or construction sites upstate, which can be far from their homes in areas where public transportation options are limited, if they are available at all.

For roughly 120,000 DACA recipients in Texas, the loss of a driver's license could be even more devastating, given the vastness of the state.

Recipients in Arizona and Georgia may face the worst circumstances. The 50,000 in those states are already largely excluded from in-state college tuition, state-funded loans and grants, and subsidized health care; they would also lose the right to drive, and in Alabama, Georgia and South Carolina, they would be barred entirely from enrolling in some colleges and universities.

Some of the estimated 280,000 beneficiaries who have attended college or graduate school have borrowed from two major lenders, Sallie Mae and Discover, which lent money to DACA recipients who could find sponsors who were United States citizens or permanent residents.

Those borrowers may now have to make loan payments without the right to work legally.

Denia Perez, who was born in Mexico and was brought to the United States when she was 11 months old, has borrowed about $40,000 from Discover to cover her living expenses at the Quinnipiac University School of Law in Connecticut. A dean's scholarship pays for her tuition, but does not cover rent, food, gas or maintenance for her 2002 Honda CRV. She also purchased a health insurance policy, required by her school, which costs about $3,000 a year.

For her final year of law school, Ms. Perez, 27, said she would borrow another $23,000, but this time from a friend. After her DACA status expires next October, she will not be able to work for a law firm in California, where she was raised and where she had planned to return to practice law. Under the terms of her Discover loans, she can defer repayment for just six months after graduating.

Ms. Perez said that if need be, she would clean houses or work as a nanny to stay afloat, the way she did as an undergraduate student. Her father is a construction worker; her mother works in food service.

"I would do what I have to do to pay my bills," she said. "I am just fully prepared to hassle and make a living and try to continue surviving in any way I can. That is what we did before DACA."

Many DACA recipients became beacons of stability in their families, and immigrant advocates said that the changes would extend beyond the recipients themselves.

Advocates for stronger immigration enforcement celebrated the changes, arguing that the resources of overburdened institutions were going to DACA recipients at the expense of American citizens and legal residents.

"You're essentially allowing parents to pass on to their children the benefits that they broke the law to obtain," said Dan Stein, the president of the Federation for American Immigration Reform, which supported Mr. Trump's decision. Mr. Stein added that the elimination of

DACA would serve as a necessary deterrent for people who consider crossing the border illegally.

Mr. Stein's views are representative of many who believe that President Barack Obama did not have the authority to create the DACA program in the first place. "Nor do states have the right to run their own immigration program for people who have no right to be in the country," he said.

But it is too soon to assume that the end of DACA will abruptly roll back all protections for its beneficiaries. The president has called on Congress to pass legislation that would make the benefits permanent, and potentially even provide a path to citizenship.

Mr. Trump said he would support such as bill, as long as it was tied to broader changes in immigration laws. He added to his rollback a six-month grace period, after which current recipients will no longer be able to renew their status. The administration immediately stopped accepting new applications.

The moves may also add pressure on states to pass their own legislation, modeled after the Dream Act, a federal bill that would give a route to citizenship to young undocumented immigrants. That proposal has languished in various forms in Congress for 16 years, and similar bills have been caught in the same political crossfire in state legislatures like New York's.

If such legislative measures fail, Ms. Gonzalez, the single mother who works at a warehouse company, will lose her status in December 2018.

Ms. Perez, the law student, has not given up her dreams of becoming a lawyer, and still thinks of her loan obligations from the perspective of someone who was months away from joining the bar. Asked to entertain the possibility that she could request debt forgiveness if she loses her legal right to work, she replied, "It's an interesting question — not sure it would hold up in court."

MIRIAM JORDAN CONTRIBUTED REPORTING.

At Least 1,900 Immigrants Were Rejected Because of Mail Problems

BY LIZ ROBBINS | JAN. 5, 2018

THREE MONTHS AFTER mail delays disrupted the lives of young immigrants whose applications to renew temporary work permits were wrongly rejected for being late, the totals are in: more than 1,900 people were affected, the United States Citizenship and Immigration Services agency said.

As Congress debates the future of the Deferred Action for Childhood Arrivals program, known as DACA, which is set to expire on March 5, the rejected applicants have been scrambling to overcome the government's error. Many have already lost their work permits, causing a cascade of consequences.

Mauricio Noroña, a lawyer for the Immigrant Community Law Center in Manhattan called the 1,900 figure, "astounding." He saw the devastating effects the mail delays had on one of his clients, whom he declined to name, saying she was afraid of repercussions from the government.

"She lost her job, lost her apartment, and is now temporarily staying with family in her home state," Mr. Noroña said. "More worrisome, our client is at risk of being placed in removal proceedings pending her DACA renewal, a process that may take months because U.S.C.I.S. didn't commit to expedite affected cases."

A spokesman for the immigration agency, Steve Blando, said that the agency has given people 33 days to resubmit their renewal forms, but would not make the applications a priority. Nor would the agency extend their current permits to cover any gaps, or even make the permit, when received, retroactive.

"There is no expedited processing for deferred action under DACA," he said in a statement. "These DACA requests will be processed in accordance with standard procedures. An individual's deferred action under the DACA policy begins the day U.S.C.I.S. approves the request and is generally valid for two years from the date of issuance."

The delayed applications were reported by The New York Times in November. Officials initially said that nothing could be done for the rejected applicants, and said the number was small. But as elected officials complained and the extent of the problem became clear, the agency reversed its position.

Some applications sat for weeks without being delivered by the Postal Service, others arrived on time at designated collection centers in Chicago, Dallas and Phoenix, but were not processed on time because of courier problems.

This week, U.S.C.I.S. said it sent letters to more than "1,700 individuals," and that more than 200 applicants resubmitted their renewals before the government invited them to do so.

HIROKO MASUIKE/THE NEW YORK TIMES

In August, shortly before President Donald Trump said he would cancel the DACA program, protesters marched near Trump Tower in favor of continuing it.

Part of the problem, immigration activists say, was that the agency imposed a "received by" deadline, instead of relying on a postmark as it does with most other immigration-related applications. In September, the Trump administration announced that it planned to end DACA on March 5 but urged Congress to find a legislative solution before then. Anyone whose permit expired before March could renew by Oct. 5.

"The fact that that many individuals were affected shows that the deadline they imposed — which we always said was too short and too arbitrary — was too short even for the government to perform its functions properly," said Camille Mackler, the director of legal initiatives for the New York Immigration Coalition.

According to U.S.C.I.S., 154,000 people were eligible to apply for renewal and 132,000 applications were received on time. According to an Oct. 18 deposition of an immigration official conducted as part of a federal lawsuit in Brooklyn, 4,000 DACA applications arrived late and were rejected.

The government is taking the blame for nearly half of those.

Hasan Shafiqullah, a lawyer for the Legal Aid Society of New York said he thought the number might even be higher.

One of his clients whose application was rejected lost his DACA protections on Dec. 1, another lost them on Dec. 23, and two more will lose theirs soon. Without DACA permits, the immigrants cannot legally work and may not be eligible for college scholarships.

According to the Center for American Progress, a liberal think tank, about 122 people have been losing their DACA permits per day, a number calculated before the extent of the mail delays were known. The full effect of the mail delays may be felt for months — or even years.

If an immigrant lives in the country illegally for any amount of time, it could have harmful repercussions, Ms. Mackler and Mr. Shafiqullah said. It could make it especially difficult for those who have turned 18 after their DACA permits expire to get green cards from employers.

"Typically DACA folks are low income, and for anyone, the inability to work is difficult, especially people living paycheck to paycheck — it can be devastating," Mr. Shafiqullah said.

DACA Participants Can Again Apply for Renewal, Immigration Agency Says

BY MATT STEVENS | JAN. 14, 2018

THE FEDERAL GOVERNMENT said on Saturday that it would resume accepting renewal requests for a program that shields from deportation young immigrants who were brought illegally to the United States as children.

In a statement, United States Citizenship and Immigration Services said that "until further notice," the Obama-era program, Deferred Action for Childhood Arrivals, known as DACA, "will be operated on the terms in place before it was rescinded" in September, when President Trump moved to end it.

The decision came after a federal judge in California issued a nationwide injunction on Tuesday ordering the Trump administration to resume the DACA program.

The agency said on Saturday that people who were previously granted deferred action under the program could request a renewal if it had expired on or after Sept. 5, 2016. People who had previously received DACA, but whose deferred action had expired before Sept. 5, 2016, cannot renew, but can instead file a new request, the agency said. It noted that the same instructions apply to anyone whose deferred action had been terminated.

But officials also said they were not accepting requests from individuals who have never been granted deferred action under DACA.

President Barack Obama created the DACA program in 2012 to give young immigrants the ability to work legally in the United States. In attempting to end it in September, President Trump argued that Mr. Obama's actions were unconstitutional and an overreach of executive power.

Critics of the president's decision to end the policy later sued the administration, saying that shutting down the program was arbitrary and done without following the proper legal procedures.

AL DRAGO FOR THE NEW YORK TIMES

A rally in Washington last month in support of the Deferred Action for Childhood Arrivals program.

The legal battle is one piece of a fierce debate in Washington. Democrats and Republicans have sparred for months about how to provide relief for about 800,000 immigrants who could face deportation.

Mr. Trump met with lawmakers on Tuesday afternoon in an hour long televised meeting to begin negotiations.

Later that day, Judge William Alsup of Federal District Court in San Francisco handed down his ruling, writing that the administration must "maintain the DACA program on a nationwide basis" as the legal challenge to the president's decision goes forward.

In his ruling, Judge Alsup laid out a road map for the government that officials appeared to follow. He said that previous beneficiaries of DACA, known as Dreamers, must be allowed to renew their status in the program, though the government would not be required to accept new applications from immigrants who had not previously submitted one.

On Sunday morning, Mr. Trump blamed Democrats for prevent-

CHILDREN AND DREAMERS **103**

ing progress on a legislative deal that would permanently legalize the young immigrants and give them an eventual path to citizenship in exchange for tougher border security and enforcement measures.

The president criticized Democratic lawmakers, some of whom have suggested that they will not support efforts to fund the government by a deadline later this week unless Congress passes the DACA legislation.

"DACA is probably dead because the Democrats don't really want it, they just want to talk and take desperately needed money away from our Military," Mr. Trump said on Twitter from his Mar-a-Lago estate in Palm Beach, Fla.

In a second tweet, Mr. Trump said that immigration legislation should include an end to the diversity visa lottery system, in which the State Department encourages diversity in immigration by holding a lottery for those wanting to come to the United States.

The president has criticized the program as a threat to the country's security even though people selected are screened in the same ways that other immigrants are. Mr. Trump has also said that the program undermines efforts by the administration to allow immigrants who have skills that will be beneficial to the United States.

"I, as President, want people coming into our Country who are going to help us become strong and great again, people coming in through a system based on MERIT," he said. "No more Lotteries! #AMERICA FIRST."

Fearing DACA's Return May Be Brief, Immigrants Rush to Renew

BY LIZ ROBBINS AND MIRIAM JORDAN | JAN. 16, 2018

FOR MARCELA ALCAIDE ELIGIO, A.P. Biology class would have to wait. First, she had some paperwork to do.

On the first day young immigrants were able to renew the permits giving them temporary protection from deportation — as ordered by a California district court last week and authorized by the United States Citizenship and Immigration Services over the holiday weekend — Ms. Alcaide, 17, had booked the first appointment of the day at the Legal Aid Society of New York.

"I had to take my chance," said Ms. Alcaide, whose permit for Deferred Action for Childhood Arrivals, or DACA, expires in May. "It's always uncertain, so you have to do it as soon as possible."

MARK ABRAMSON FOR THE NEW YORK TIMES

Hasan Shafiqullah, the director of the immigration unit at the Legal Aid Society of New York, takes Marcela Alcaide Eligio's photograph for her DACA renewal application.

In Los Angeles, people started lining up at 2:30 in the morning on Tuesday for appointments to renew DACA applications at the Coalition for Humane Immigrant Rights of Los Angeles. The group only had 20 slots available, and by 8 a.m., staffers had to start turning people away and begin scheduling them for Thursday.

"I wanted to take this opportunity while the window lasts," said Mario Hernandez, 29, who was whisked across the Mexico-United States border when he was a 1-year-old and raised in Los Angeles.

Hours later, his sense of urgency seemed prescient. The Department of Justice filed a notice of appeal on Tuesday afternoon in the U.S. Court of Appeals for the Ninth Circuit, saying it intended to ask the Supreme Court later in the week to review the Federal District Court's ruling, which had enjoined the federal government from ending the DACA program, as it had planned.

With their fates split in the courts, in the halls of Congress, and, seemingly, the White House, DACA recipients across the country scrambled to do what was in their power.

Lawyers were urging their clients to apply as soon as they could, given the short window of opportunity that only seemed to get shorter on Tuesday. "We're trying to schedule events as fast as we can," said Camille Mackler, the director of legal initiatives at the New York Immigration Coalition, an advocacy group.

In New York, the Mayor's Office of Immigrant Affairs was partnering with CUNY Citizenship Now! to offer two free clinics on Thursday and next Tuesday, while Make the Road New York, another immigrant advocacy group in the city, had filled all its slots for three Saturday events.

In Phoenix, a community organizing and advocacy group, Puente Arizona, had already helped prepare six applications on Monday, even though it was a federal holiday. On Tuesday the applicants only needed to put them in the mail — with a tracking number to avoid any problems with the United States Postal Service that plagued the renewal program in the fall, when more than 1,900 applicants were rejected for being late because of mail delays.

In some cities, though, the DACA push in response to immigration authorities reopening renewal applications was slower than others. Geoffrey Hoffman, the director of the immigration clinic at the University of Houston Law Center, said on Tuesday that the clinic had received only a handful of inquiries from DACA recipients.

"It's been very sparse," Mr. Hoffman said on Tuesday. "I would say there's still a fair amount of uncertainty with regard to whether these applications will be accepted," he added.

But another legal services group in Houston said it had received 50 to 100 emails, calls and walk-in consultations since the federal judge's injunction last week.

On Sept. 5, when the Trump administration announced that it was phasing out the DACA program, which grants the deportation protection and work permits to young people who were brought to the United States illegally by their parents as children, it allowed only those recipients whose benefits expired between Sept. 5, 2017 and March 5, 2018 to renew for a final two years.

According to the immigration agency, 132,000 out of the 154,000 people eligible to renew applied in the fall. But this time, anyone whose permit had expired since Sept. 5, 2016 or was canceled at any time could apply.

The immigration agency said that anyone whose permit expired in the next 120 to 150 days could reapply. It historically has accepted people as many as six months out.

In California, Luis Cruz's permit expires in June, so after the administration canceled the DACA program in September, he stopped saving money from his job at a communications firm for the $495 application fee. That changed with last week's court ruling.

The Coalition for Humane Immigrant Rights, known as Chirla, said it would cover the cost, to Mr. Cruz's gratitude. "It's done, sealed in an envelope and about to be express-mailed," he said.

The lawyer for Ms. Alcaide in New York, Hasan Shafiqullah, the director of the immigration unit at the Legal Aid Society, said he

MARK ABRAMSON FOR THE NEW YORK TIMES

Marcela Alcaide Eligio reads over the paperwork for her renewal application. Her mother paid her $495 fee.

sent an email to 950 former DACA clients on Monday, explaining the renewal process. He got only 10 responses.

By the end of Tuesday, he had sent out four applications via FedEx, paid for by Legal Aid in an effort to avoid the earlier mail problems.

Mr. Shafiqullah said that perhaps some of the unit's clients did not need legal assistance with their applications because they have renewed twice already and were familiar with the process. For Ms. Alcaide, who came from Mexico when she was 2 years old, it was her first renewal. Her mother gave her the application fee from her savings from cleaning houses.

"It's really exciting because I don't have to fear anything else for two more years," Ms. Alcaide said.

Now, she added that she will be able to apply for colleges in New York with more assurance that she can earn money to pay tuition.

But Mr. Shafiqullah had to caution her, as he has been doing for his other clients. The afternoon decision from the Department of Justice underscored why.

"The fact that this has started isn't a guarantee that it will continue," he told her across the desk, "but we're hoping that those who manage to apply in time, even if there is an injunction, if you get your foot in the door, then they will honor that."

LIZ ROBBINS REPORTED FROM NEW YORK; MIRIAM JORDAN FROM LOS ANGELES. MANNY FERNANDEZ CONTRIBUTED REPORTING FROM HOUSTON, REBEKAH ZEMANSKY FROM PHOENIX.

Trump Says He Is Open to a Path to Citizenship for 'Dreamers'

BY MAGGIE HABERMAN, KATIE ROGERS AND MICHAEL D. SHEAR | JAN. 24, 2018

WASHINGTON — President Trump said on Wednesday that he is open to a path to citizenship after 10 to 12 years for hundreds of thousands of undocumented immigrants brought to the United States as children, days after rejecting a bipartisan plan with that as its centerpiece.

Mr. Trump once again seemed to undercut his administration's message, telling reporters at the White House that he would allow the young immigrants, known as Dreamers, to "morph into" citizens over a period of time.

The reporters had gathered for a briefing from a senior official detailing the administration's plans to stick to a restrictive immigration agenda when the president dropped in unprompted, shortly before departing for Davos, Switzerland, pre-empting the official.

"Over a period of 10 to 12 years," Mr. Trump said, "somebody does a great job, they work hard — that gives incentive to do a great job. Whatever they're doing, if they do a great job, I think it's a nice thing to have the incentive of, after a period of years, being able to become a citizen."

In September, Mr. Trump ended an Obama-era program, called Deferred Action for Childhood Arrivals, or DACA, saying it was an illegal assertion of executive authority by his predecessor. But even as Mr. Trump's actions threatened nearly 700,000 young immigrants with deportation when the program expires March 5, he has urged Congress to find a permanent solution that could allow them to live and work in the country legally.

In addition to suggesting a pathway to citizenship for the Dreamers, Mr. Trump said that he would request $25 billion to build a wall along the United States border with Mexico, though he said he would build it "way under budget." He also said that his plan would include a request for $5 billion for additional security measures along the border.

The fate of the Dreamers is at the center of a furious stalemate in Congress, where Republicans and Democrats are struggling to find a compromise. Mr. Trump's positions have been difficult to discern, vacillating between his expressions of sympathy for the DACA recipients and his hard-line demands for a crackdown on illegal immigrants.

Mr. Trump campaigned for the presidency with nativist rhetoric that assailed the threat from outsiders, especially Mexicans and Muslims. As president, he quickly tried to impose a travel ban on predominantly Muslim countries and gave immigration agents more authority to round up undocumented immigrants.

But he also once said that he wanted "a bill of love" to address the fate of the DACA recipients.

Senator Tom Cotton, Republican of Arkansas, who is a hard-line conservative on immigration issues, reiterated that any deal on immigration would have to include Republican demands for tougher enforcement on immigration, saying on Twitter that "it must be done responsibly, guaranteeing a secure & lawful border & ending chain migration, to mitigate the negative side effects of codifying DACA."

Mr. Trump's remarks drew support from Lindsey Graham, Republican of South Carolina, who has in recent weeks been at the forefront of efforts to reach an immigration deal. Mr. Graham had been one of the architects of the bipartisan plan rejected by Mr. Trump.

"President Trump's support for a pathway to citizenship will help us get strong border security measures as we work to modernize a broken immigration system," Mr. Graham said in a statement. "Finally, with this statement we are on track to solving the immigration problem, which is the political key to rebuilding our military."

Senator Richard J. Durbin, Democrat of Illinois, who in 2001 first sponsored the "DREAM Act" to provide legal status to the young immigrants, also praised the president. "The President is headed in the right direction here," Mr. Durbin wrote Wednesday evening on Twitter.

As the Trump administration struggled in recent days to produce an on-message stance on immigration, Mr. Trump has kept largely out of sight, as his chief of staff, John F. Kelly, coordinated with Republican leaders while they worked with Democrats to reopen the government after a three-day shutdown.

Mr. Kelly and Stephen Miller, Mr. Trump's senior policy adviser, are immigration hard-liners and are major proponents of the kind of "legislative framework" that earlier in the day Sarah Huckabee Sanders, the White House press secretary, said the administration would release on Monday that would be intended to emphasize conservative demands for tougher immigration enforcement and border protection. Neither Mr. Kelly nor Mr. Miller accompanied the president to the World Economic Forum in Davos.

Within hours, Mr. Trump's off-the-cuff comments to reporters seemed, again, to suggest flexibility. But his remarks sent the White House staff scrambling in what one official called a "fire drill." After delaying the briefing for nearly an hour, Mr. Trump's aides decided to postpone it until Thursday as they tried to reconcile their plans with the president's words.

Mr. Trump, once again, said he will insist on an end to the diversity lottery system, which encourages immigration from a variety of countries. Mr. Trump referred to the program as a "broken system" that brings the wrong kind of people into the United States. He said that he wanted to negotiate an end to so-called chain migration, but said he would work to allow nuclear families to stay together.

Despite the president's pledge to the Dreamers, his administration cracked down earlier Wednesday on so-called sanctuary cities. The Justice Department asked the 23 jurisdictions across the country to furnish documents proving that they had not kept information from federal immigration authorities. The department's move caused several Democratic mayors from some of the country's largest cities to boycott a White House meeting with Mr. Trump.

"Protecting criminal aliens from federal immigration authorities defies common sense and undermines the rule of law," Attorney General Jeff Sessions said in a statement. "Enough is enough."

The protest against the letter and Mr. Sessions's comments added a local dimension to the roiling national debate. Mitch Landrieu, the mayor of New Orleans and the president of the United States Conference of Mayors, said on Wednesday at a news conference in Washington that he saw the Justice Department's move as an "attack," and that he could not "in good conscience" attend the White House meeting.

Sanctuary cities, which generally refuse to hold people on immigration agents' behalf without a warrant from a judge, have pushed back hard over the past year on the administration's attempts to force them to abandon their stance by cutting off federal funding to them. Some, like Chicago, have filed lawsuits against the Justice Department.

"President Trump shouldn't invite us to the White House for a meeting on infrastructure and three hours before issue the equivalent of what are arrest warrants for standing up for what we believe in and, by the way, what America believes in," Mayor Rahm Emanuel of Chicago said.

Mr. Sessions has taken a hard line on the issue since his days as an Alabama senator. Since Mr. Trump took office, both men have focused on sanctuary cities, accusing such places of flouting the law and helping convicted criminals evade deportation.

Armed with the news that several Democratic mayors had declined an invitation to the White House, Mr. Trump again returned to a partisan stance on immigration.

"The mayors who choose to boycott this event have put the needs of criminal, illegal immigrants over law-abiding America," Mr. Trump said at the event, held hours before he dropped in on reporters.

As the president ended his conversation with reporters and prepared to leave for Switzerland, he jokingly suggested that he would like a deal on immigration in place by the time he returns.

Mr. Trump is scheduled to arrive back at the White House on Friday night.

KATIE BENNER AND SHERYL GAY STOLBERG CONTRIBUTED REPORTING.

Most Americans Want Legal Status for 'Dreamers.' These People Don't.

BY MIRIAM JORDAN | JAN. 25, 2018

FOR PAV STERRY of Columbus, Ohio, legalizing any undocumented immigrants — even those who came as children without a choice in the matter — is just plain wrong.

Huy Pham of St. Paul believes any concessions for the so-called Dreamers will unleash another tidal wave of illegal immigration. And Daniel Cotts of Phoenix regards "blanket amnesty" for them as unfair to foreigners who languish for years waiting to come here the legal way.

Poll after poll has shown that a large majority of Americans support protections for young immigrants who were brought to the United States illegally as children.

TIM GRUBER FOR THE NEW YORK TIMES

Huy Pham in front of his parents' home in St. Paul. When he was a toddler, his family entered the United States legally as refugees from Vietnam, and he opposes granting legal status to undocumented immigrants.

Yet there remains a slice of the American public for whom the idea of legalizing an undocumented immigrant has not gotten better with age.

They do not dispute that most of the immigrants are eager and hardworking and did not choose their station in life. But for these voters, that is all beside the point.

"I think DACA recipients should be given a few months to get their affairs in order and return to their home countries," said Ms. Sterry, 58, a former math teacher, referring to the Obama-era program, Deferred Action for Childhood Arrivals, that President Trump has ended but which could be revived or replaced in a congressional deal.

And to those who contend that the young immigrants would be marooned in a country they do not remember, Ms. Sterry says: "Parents and children can all go home together."

Less than a quarter of American voters, and in some polls as few as one in 10, share Ms. Sterry's beliefs. But they show how the country's conflicted emotions about undocumented immigrants have stymied legislation for more than a decade, polarizing both parties and most recently leading to the short-lived government shutdown that still did not settle the issue.

Their counterparts on the liberal side are the progressives who are upset with Senate Democrats like Chuck Schumer, the minority leader, for allowing the government to reopen without a guarantee of protection for DACA recipients, known as Dreamers.

On the Republican side, moderates are feeling the pull of hard-line members who want any legalization bill to incorporate significant changes to immigration enforcement, including measures Democrats generally oppose, such as funding for a border wall, a sharp reduction in overall migration, and a shift to merit-based admissions from a family-based system that critics call "chain migration."

President Trump has repeatedly expressed support for legalizing DACA recipients — on Wednesday, he said he was open to granting them a path to citizenship "at some point in the future, over a period of 10 to 12 years." But he, too, has felt the pull from people in his administration who objected to the program, which was created by former President Barack Obama in 2012.

In announcing the end of DACA last September, Attorney General Jeff Sessions called it a "unilateral executive amnesty" that had encouraged more illegal immigration and "denied jobs to hundreds of thousands of Americans by allowing those same jobs to go to illegal aliens."

Lars Larson, a syndicated conservative talk-show host based in Portland, Ore., said that 10 to 15 percent of his callers consider DACA recipients lawbreakers and want to give them "nothing at all."

"I point out that philosophically, I agree with them, but practically this needs to be resolved," he said, by granting permission to stay only in exchange for tougher enforcement measures. "Show us that you are bringing something of value."

In interviews, voters who oppose legalization said that they felt the government was being held hostage by sympathizers of the young immigrants. Most were resigned to the possibility that a deal could happen, and said that they could live with it if conservatives came away with significant new immigration controls.

Still, several invoked the law signed by President Ronald Reagan in 1986, which granted 2.7 million people amnesty while tightening security at the Mexican border and adding strict penalties for employers who hired undocumented workers. Though it promised to reduce illegal immigration, the number of undocumented people has grown since then to an estimated 11 million.

"Granting legal status to Dreamers could potentially cause a domino effect in which other families bring young children, hoping that in time their children will be granted legal status," said Jaclyn Haak, 19, a chemical engineering student at the University of Minnesota.

She acknowledged that many DACA recipients are contributing to the economy, but said that this did not mean that legalizing them was in the country's best interest. She said it could undermine job prospects for Americans, echoing a concern by immigration restrictionist groups.

For Joe Kleve, 21, a senior at St. Mary's University of Minnesota in Winona, the argument that the young immigrants had been brought by their parents held no weight.

What if someone's parents were caught sneaking their whole family into a movie without paying, he asked. "Are they going to just kick the parents out?"

For Mr. Pham, 39, the issue was personal. He, too, arrived in the United States as a toddler, as a legally admitted refugee from Vietnam. But until his family could find American sponsors, they were parked in a refugee camp overseas for more than a year.

"If we can do it the legal way, so can they," said Mr. Pham, an information technology consultant. "We don't have to be creating new programs or giving them preferential treatment."

The voters opposing legalization were often well-informed about some of the details of the immigration debate, such as E-Verify, an electronic worker-verification system that many Republicans want to make mandatory for employers, and the diversity visa lottery, which admits up to 50,000 foreigners a year who must be vetted, but do not need any special skills or family ties to the United States. Proposals to eliminate the lottery have been circulating for years.

At the same time, a few of those interviewed held to common misconceptions about the young immigrants. Some said the immigrants should not be allowed to become legal if they had not tried to do so before DACA was created. But it is almost impossible for people to secure green cards once they have been here illegally for several years.

Others expressed the sentiment that the immigrants' parents should have gotten "in line," though for many foreigners, a legal pathway into the country exists only if they have special skills or relatives in the United States who are citizens.

While these voters remain in the minority, support is not absolute among the majority who want to legalize the young immigrants.

In a CNN poll last week, 84 percent of those surveyed said they supported legal status for Dreamers. But when given a choice between keeping the government open and passing DACA legislation, 56 percent of those polled said it was more important to keep the government open and only 34 percent said a legalization bill was more important, with the rest believing they were equally important or having no opinion. The lack of firm support for the shutdown most likely contributed to Democrats' decision to end it on Monday.

And for those who disdain legalization, that feeling is not always absolute, either. When pressed on whether deportations of the young immigrants should begin — a distinct possibility if no deal is reached — some hedged their opposition.

"They'd be sent back to countries they have no connection to, don't know anything about — it's a very complex situation," said Mr. Cotts, a lawyer, adding that he would like lawmakers to "find a middle ground," perhaps one that prohibits the immigrants from becoming citizens with voting rights.

Mr. Pham suggested letting the immigrants stay, but expelling all those who commit crimes, or even get speeding tickets. "If they're here already, and they are contributing to society, leave them alone," he said. He said he did not want them becoming citizens, but then added he would entertain the thought for those who served in the military.

Ms. Sterry, however, stuck to her stance. "Let's not pretend this is only about the children," she said. Once the young immigrants are legalized, support will mount for legalizing their parents, too, she believed.

When asked about what it felt like to take an unpopular position, Ms. Sterry responded: "I don't care about being popular. Amnesty is wrong."

CHRISTINA CAPECCHI CONTRIBUTED REPORTING FROM MINNEAPOLIS, AND REBEKAH ZEMANSKY FROM PHOENIX.

The Americans Left Behind by Deportation

OPINION | BY KARLA CORNEJO VILLAVICENCIO | FEB. 28, 2018

IN THE FALL, I traveled to rural Ohio to meet with the children of a man who had been recently deported to Mexico, even though he was considered a model citizen by his neighbors and had no criminal record beyond driving without a license. I had seen video footage of his three young boys and little girl saying goodbye to him at the airport. They looked like orphaned bear cubs, wandering around aimlessly in the terminal, their faces frozen in fear.

Eric, the oldest at 14, is in the eighth grade and wants the local Wendy's to make an exception to its minimum age requirement so he can work there. "I'm the man of the house now," he told me. When their father left, so did the only member of the family who could drive. Eric walks several miles to the grocery store and returns carrying heavy bags of food even in the snow. Their mother, who is also undocumented, is now the family's sole source of income and works long hours at a factory, so Eric has to come straight home from school to take care of his younger siblings. (He had to scrap plans to try out for the wrestling team.)

Edwin, 12, has nightmares about his father and crawls into his mother's bed almost every night. Classmates taunt him that they hope his mother gets deported, too. Anuar, 10, who calms himself by doing equations in his head, brought me his report card with a perfect 100 in math. Elsiy, 6, has not been eating well since her father's been gone.

America's historic uneasiness with interracial marriage and mixed-race children has found a new incarnation in the persecution of families with mixed legal status. There are nearly six million citizen children who live with at least one undocumented parent, and perhaps millions of other Americans who are married to undocumented immigrants. Reports are multiplying of Immigration and Customs Enforcement agents picking up immigrants at their green card couple interviews, while their American spouses are left speechless and powerless. The Trump administration's aggressive detention and removal of undocumented immigrants is not only inhumane in its treatment of immigrants, but a direct attack on the rights and well-being of their American family members.

I recently met Jim Chuquirima, a 16-year-old American citizen whose mother is undocumented. He is bespectacled, painfully shy and builds computers out of spare parts that his mother, Nelly Cumbicos, buys him. Ms. Cumbicos is a movie-star-beautiful single mother from Ecuador who had sworn off men before she met Ramón Muñiz, a roofer and die-hard union man who lived on the first floor of the multifamily home in Meriden, Conn., where Jim and Nelly rented the third floor. He would fix Nelly's car, pick Jim up from school while she was at work and leave unsigned love letters on the windshield of her car. They married in their home on Halloween in 2015.

An American citizen, he insisted in 2015 that she let him petition for her green card, even though she was afraid it would put ICE on her trail. She was right: When ICE became aware of Ms. Cumbico's whereabouts, it located a deportation order from more than a decade before that she says she had never received because it was sent to a wrong address. ICE gave her a temporary stay on Feb. 5 only to inexplicably rescind it four days later. Like a botched execution, it left the family newly traumatized. Their legal fees have nearly bankrupted them. Her deportation is set for Wednesday.

"I feel like this is my fault," Mr. Muñiz said. "I put her in danger, but all I wanted was to protect her. I'm lost without her."

In the early 1900s, American women who married foreigners lost their citizenship. Those laws are off the books now. But does that mean American citizens have the constitutional right to be protected from the deportation of an immediate family member? Lower courts haven't thought so. In one case, the United States Court of Appeals for the Third Circuit decided the deportation of an American-born infant's parents didn't violate her right to grow up in this country because either her parents could surrender her to foster care in America before they left or she could leave with them and return to the United States as an adult. The Court of Appeals for the 10th Circuit has declared that a parent's deportation has only "incidental impact" on a child. Studies, however, have shown that children with parents who are under threat of deportation or have been deported fall into depression and anxiety and are more likely to have behavioral problems and to experience drastically decreased academic performance. Couples who are separated by oceans are very likely to end up divorced.

The Supreme Court has historically declared that it is "intolerable" to force a citizen to choose between two constitutional rights. But what then of the American families of deportees? Isn't the Trump administration forcing them to make a terrible choice, between either staying in the United States and having their families rived in two, or forfeiting their lives in America so that they can keep their families intact?

I, too, had to worry about this dilemma. I am the child of undocumented immigrants from Ecuador who brought me to this country when I was 5. I am the American dream incarnate, with an Ivy League education and a book deal. Now I am married to an American citizen, but there is no guarantee that my spouse's status will shield me from deportation.

For my own green card interview, I wore the collared pink silk J. Crew dress I wore to our wedding. I dress glamorously and wear a face full of designer makeup in any situation where I might be detained, out of pride and defiance. But this interview was not bait to detain me, the way interviews have been for so many less fortunate immigrants.

"There is nothing I wanted more than to be able to protect you from your nightmares," my partner told me after we'd read about the tragedy that had befallen other citizen-undocumented couples. "I wasn't thinking so much about the literal, legal rights that the green card would afford; I was thinking about what do I need to do to keep my family safe, and that meant making sure we could be a family. It was such a low bar."

I got my green card. Our marriage is real. My guilt is as well. It is so hard to imagine that Ramón's desire to keep Nelly safe provoked the exact opposite result.

Short of comprehensive immigration reform, which seems so unlikely these days, there are ways to end these inhumane deportations. In February 2017, John Kelly, then the secretary of homeland security, issued a memo essentially doing away with enforcement priorities for ICE, which generally called for not targeting undocumented immigrants if they did not have serious criminal records. The Kelly memo made all undocumented immigrants targets — even if they had spotless records, and even if they had spouses or children who were citizens. A return to Obama-era priorities that focused on criminals and security risks would restore some level of compassion to enforcement in the short term. Though far from the best solution, that would at least protect the rights of citizens.

Unless protecting American citizens was never the point of any of this.

KARLA CORNEJO VILLAVICENCIO IS A GRADUATE STUDENT IN AMERICAN STUDIES AT YALE.

CHAPTER 4

Individuals and Communities

Every immigrant's story is different, but many can relate to some amount of homesickness, culture shock, language barriers and unfriendly treatment from locals. As they find themselves separated from family and without the support systems they once had in their countries of origin, immigrants often form strong communities among themselves, supporting each other and sharing useful knowledge about their new homes. These communities become engrained as vital parts of the towns and cities where they have formed, enriching the cultural diversity of these areas.

Working to Help Irish Immigrants Stay, Legally

BY MARVINE HOWE | NOV. 27, 1988

ON A RECENT EVENING in a basement in Woodside, Queens, half a dozen volunteers sat under defiant green-and-white posters that read, "Legalize The Irish."

The volunteers, working for the Irish Immigration Reform Movement, a lobbying and advisory group founded in Woodside last year, were answering calls on the hotline and talking about an amendment signed into law by President Reagan last week. The legislation, called an Amendment in the Nature of a Substitute for HR5115 and introduced by Congressmen Peter W. Rodino Jr. of New Jersey and Romano L. Mazzoli of Kentucky, could mean as many as 30,000 new visas for Irish immigrants.

President Ronald Reagan.

Many of these immigrants will wind up in New York City, which already has the largest Irish community in the country and where about 70,000 Irish immigrants have recently settled. About 150,000 Irish immigrants came to New York as students or tourists over the last six years and stayed on as undocumented aliens.

"The fight isn't over; this is just the first step," said Pat Hurley, a founding member of the Movement. Mr. Hurley said the group would resume lobbying even before the new Congress convenes, working closely with established Irish-American organizations like the Ancient Order of Hibernians.

AMNESTY IS SOUGHT

The Movement, which addresses day-to-day problems of Irish immigrants through its hotline, hopes above all to secure amnesty for all illegal aliens who were not covered by the 1986 Immigration Reform and Control Act. It also seeks "corrective legislation" to provide a large annual quota of immigrant visas on a nonpreference basis for the 36 countries, including Ireland, adversely affected by the 1965 Immigration and Nationality Act.

"The new legislation is a small victory but it has raised the hopes of undocumented Irish," said Linda Mc Evatt, a legal secretary and a volunteer in the organization who received a green card in 1986. "Being illegal is nonexistence; you've got no job security, no medical insurance, no right to open a bank account and are an open target for landlords and employers."

The Irish feel they have been doubly disfavored by recent United States immigration laws. The 1965 act raised quotas from countries that had been previously disadvantaged, namely those in Asia and Latin America, and established a system under which an immigrant with family in the United States was given preference.

This proved prejudicial to European countries like Ireland, whose emigration had slowed. Official statistics showed a drastic reduction in the number of legal Irish immigrants, with more than 70,000 coming to this country in the decade 1956-65, compared with only 10,000 plus in 1976-85.

The 1986 reform provided amnesty for illegal aliens who could prove they had stayed in the United States continuously since 1982, but again the Irish lost out because the new wave of immigration from Ireland came only after that year, spurred on largely by an economic crisis in Ireland.

The State Department listed 36 countries "disadvantaged" by the 1965 Immigration Act because they could not benefit from family preferences. Congressman Brian J. Donnelly of Massachusetts introduced a clause into the 1986 Immigration Act providing for a lottery to give these countries more visas. Under this scheme, 10,000 nonpreferential visas were allocated on a first-come, first-served basis to applications sent to a Washington post office box on Jan. 21, 1987.

Of a total of 1.5 million pieces of mail received in the lottery, 200,000 of the earliest applications came from Irish citizens, winning 4,161 of the 10,000 visas. The explanation given for this Irish "luck" is that the Irish felt the most pressing need to emigrate and were better organized, getting more applications in sooner than the others.

3 PARTS TO LEGISLATION

The new legislation, which was passed by the Senate on Oct. 5 and by the House of Representative on Oct 21, and signed by President Reagan on Nov. 15, contains three parts:

- A reactivation of the Donnelly project. Now under the new law, the Justice Department will allocate the first 30,000 visas to applicants remaining from the 1987 lottery. A reserve list of 15,000 names, 10,000 of them Irish, has already been established, and another reserve list of 15,000 names will come from the same pool.

- A new lottery that would allocate another 20,000 visas over a two years, starting October 1989, randomly rather than on a first-come, first-served basis. Under this measure, applicants may apply from 140 countries that are considered "under-represented" — those with fewer than 25 percent of the visas that were available to them last year. Ireland is among this group.

- An extension to December 1989 of temporary H-1 visas for foreign nurses. Such visas expire this year. The measure was a short-term way to address the critical need for nurses in New York and many other cities.

IRELAND 'PLEASED'

Daragh O' Criodain, a spokesman for the Irish Embassy in Washington, said the Irish Government was "very pleased" about the legislation after it was passed.

Gary Galanis, press secretary for Rep. Donnelly, said Mr. Donnelly would "pursue his efforts for a more comprehensive reform next year." He called the Irish Immigration Reform Movement "one of the better organized lobbying groups."

The organization, which has 17 branches in other Irish communities around the country, has supported its lobbying action through fundraisers and raffles. Recently, however, it won a $30,000 grant from the City of New York for its activities as an immigration advisory group.

With Affluent Chinese Moving In, a Press War Begins to Heat Up

BY DAVID W. CHEN | APRIL 16, 1995

IT HAS BEEN A VERY, very good year for Li Yung and his New Jersey China Times.

On Jan. 1, the Chinese-language weekly published its first issue, with a press run of 5,000 copies. On April 1, that figure hit 20,000, distributed free at 56 restaurants, banks and supermarkets throughout New Jersey.

"No one thought that we would do so well so fast," Mr. Li said. "But I think it shows how interested the readers are in community news."

Mr. Li is not alone in his surprise, or, apparently, in his success.

Just a few years ago, New Jersey residents hungry for Chinese-language news had to drive to New York for papers that paid little, if any, attention to their home state. Now, they can flip through the likes of Sino Monthly New Jersey, New Creation Connection, Neo Asian American Times and Mr. Li's New Jersey China Times.

These publications make no bones about focusing on New Jersey. They solicit local advertising, report on real estate, education and investment opportunities and list cultural events. (The Neo Asian American Times is somewhat political, supporting Taiwan's opposition Democratic Progressive Party.) By contrast, the New York papers pay more attention to what's happening in China, Taiwan and Hong Kong than to local news.

This proliferation of Chinese-language publications reflects the speedy growth of Chinese communities around the state. Between 1980 and 1990, according to the census, the state's ethnic Chinese population increased from 23,492 to 59,094, or 152 percent. (Even more strikingly, the number who identified themselves as Chinese speakers grew from 3,358 in 1980 to 47,334 in 1990.) In Middlesex and Somerset Counties, the number of Chinese residents more than tripled over the same period; in Edison, which is fast becoming a hub of suburban Chinese, the figure climbed from 485 in 1980 to 2,561 in 1990.

For the most part, these are not struggling immigrants; though many are new to America, they tend to be reasonably well off, and they have come to settle. Some are professionals who work at Bell Labs or various Taiwanese companies in the state. Some are former Chinatown or Flushing residents who work in New York City but want more space and safety.

"In New Jersey, the house is bigger, the education is better, and you don't need to worry about parking," said Annie Yee, a mortgage broker who recently moved to Edison after 20 years in Queens. "You don't have to go to New York to eat or shop. You have everything you need in New Jersey."

When it comes to news, New Jersey's Chinese have several choices.

New Creation Connection of Edison prints about 20,000 copies each week and distributes them free to restaurants, churches and groceries. Founded in 1991 by the New Jersey First Chinese Baptist Church of Edison, the 24-page tabloid contains articles on local business, music and education, as well as short fiction, international news and a "Practical English" lesson.

"We picked Edison because the Chinese population is growing so fast, and we felt it would be the next Chinatown," said Micah Wong, the paper's marketing director.

Sino Monthly New Jersey is an independent magazine published in East Brunswick. It started in 1991 as a 16-page black-and-white publication with a paid circulation of 8,000 and a total of 30 ads. In the most recent issue, there were 88 pages in color and 200 ads for a paid circulation of more than 16,000, said Ivy Lee, the magazine's editor.

The magazine offers special monthly reports on topics like immigration, real estate and demographics. It also devotes space to entertainment news, business reports, monthly columns and restaurant reviews.

Mr. Li's New Jersey China Times takes a similar approach. In recent months, the 12-page broadsheet has featured articles on everything from Chinese who plunk down cash to buy houses to whether complicated or simplified Chinese characters should be taught in local Chinese schools.

The newspaper is actually produced in Manhattan, but its main offices are in Edison and Fair Lawn, and its circulation is limited to New Jersey.

Then there's the Neo Asian American Times. The Queens-based weekly, established in 1991, used to circulate only in New York, but now distributes 30 percent of its 10,000 print run to New Jersey. Two weeks ago, the 12-page paper switched to daily publication, combining New York and New Jersey news with international news from Taiwan's Liberty Times newspaper.

Of course, going beyond Volume 1, No. 1 is not easy. Witness New Hua Monthly, an Edison-based magazine begun in December 1993 to great fanfare, including congratulatory notes from then-Governor Jim Florio and Senator Frank Lautenberg. It folded after three issues.

And there is still stiff competition from established New York dailies such as World Journal and Sing Tao, not to mention a plethora of trade publications and community newsletters.

But the New Jersey papers are confident they've found a niche: well-to-do suburbanites who care more about community events and good schools than homeland politics.

Readers and advertisers seem to like what they see.

Stephen Tsai is a partner with Wong, Tsai and Fleming, an Edison law firm that was founded last year and specializes in serving the Chinese community. So far, his firm has advertised in Sino Monthly New Jersey and World Journal.

"The fact that newspapers are popping up all over the place is a sign of the tremendous growth of the Asian community," he said. "There's a need for these publications."

Black Groups Seeking Asylum for a Teenager From Guinea

BY JOHN FILES | MARCH 14, 2004

THE CONGRESSIONAL BLACK CAUCUS and the N.A.A.C.P. are calling for the Department of Homeland Security to grant asylum to a teenager from Guinea who was held in adult jails and other detention centers for more than three years during a legal struggle to remain in the United States.

The youth, Malik Jarno, now 19, arrived alone from Guinea in January 2001 at Dulles International Airport. His case has become a symbol of the difficulties encountered by thousands of young immigrants who arrive unaccompanied each year and are detained.

The Congressional Black Caucus, in a letter to Asa Hutchinson, the under secretary for border and transportation security, said, "We strongly urge you to intervene personally in this case by directing that the department stipulate to a grant of asylum for Malik."

The letter, which was sent Friday, was written by Representative Donald M. Payne, Democrat of New Jersey, and signed by all 39 members of the caucus.

Hilary O. Shelton, director to the Washington bureau of the N.A.A.C.P., also wrote a letter to Mr. Hutchinson, urging Mr. Jarno's asylum.

The case prompted members of Congress and human rights groups to press Mr. Hutchinson to release Mr. Jarno. Because Mr. Jarno was not considered a security threat, officials said, Mr. Hutchinson ordered him released from jail in December.

Mr. Jarno, described by his lawyers as mentally retarded, is now living at a refugee shelter in York, Pa., pending his asylum request. He fled his country seeking sanctuary from political persecution that left his family dead, his lawyers say.

The letter from the caucus said there was evidence "that Malik will likely be persecuted in Guinea on account of his father's political opinion being imputed to him, his membership in this prominent family and his mental condition."

A spokesman for the Department of Homeland Security, Bill Strassberger, said that the letters would be reviewed and that Mr. Hutchinson would respond to them.

"The secretary is empathetic to the situation and wants to ensure that Mr. Jarno gets a fair hearing," Mr. Strassberger said.

A lawyer for Mr. Jarno, Christopher Nugent, said he would most likely be scheduled for an asylum hearing in the next few weeks.

In 2000, Mr. Jarno traveled to France from Guinea, in West Africa, after his father, a Muslim cleric and political activist, was killed by government forces. He was detained by immigration officials when he tried to enter the United States with a fake French passport.

The Immigration and Naturalization Service said Mr. Jarno, who speaks French and Puhlar, a West African language, was not a minor, contrary to his birth certificate.

Responsibility for detained immigrant children — about 500 remain in detention — fell to the Department of Health and Human Services after the Immigration and Naturalization Service was absorbed by the Homeland Security Department in 2002.

Last year, the human rights group Amnesty International, which has pushed for less restrictive placements or foster homes for children who are awaiting determination of their legal status, found that foreign children fleeing violence and persecution in their home countries were often improperly detained for months in bleak detention centers in the United States without access to lawyers or psychological services.

Activists and ICE Face Off Over Detained Immigrant Leader

BY LIZ ROBBINS | JAN. 12, 2018

AN ESCALATING LEGAL BATTLE played out on Friday in the case of Ravi Ragbir, an immigrant rights activist whose detention on Thursday by federal immigration authorities sparked protests that led to the arrest of 18 people, including members of the New York City Council.

Mr. Ragbir, 53, the executive director of the New Sanctuary Coalition of New York City, had shown up for a check-in with Immigration and Customs Enforcement on Thursday morning, at the Jacob K. Javits Federal Building in Lower Manhattan. When officials told him that he was going to be detained and deported, Mr. Ragbir fainted, his wife, Amy Gottlieb, said.

That is when events turned chaotic.

TODD HEISLER/THE NEW YORK TIMES

The Rev. Juan Carlos Ruiz, of the New Sanctuary Coalition of NYC, hugs Amy Gottlieb, whose husband, Ravi Ragbir, an immigrant rights activist, was detained by ICE pending deportation.

His lawyer from New York University Immigrant Rights Clinic, Alina Das, said that as he was regaining consciousness she argued that she was still pursuing legal remedies for Mr. Ragbir. She said that Scott Mechkowski, the assistant field office director for ICE, dismissed her arguments and had officers handcuff Mr. Ragbir.

An ambulance called for Mr. Ragbir was met with angry protesters as it left the federal building. The protest extended onto Broadway and toward City Hall and council members Ydanis Rodriguez and Jumaane D. Williams were among the 18 arrested.

Ms. Gottlieb rode to Lower Manhattan Hospital of New York-Presbyterian in the ambulance with Mr. Ragbir, she said. There, Ms. Gottlieb said, she was told to get out of the ambulance, which then left with Mr. Ragbir inside. Ms. Gottlieb learned later that it had taken him to a hospital devoid of protesters, Bellevue Hospital Center, for evaluation. From there, the New York Police Department provided an escort for federal immigration vehicles to the Holland Tunnel; unbeknown to his wife, lawyer and supporters, Mr. Ragbir was soon on a plane to Miami, where he was placed in a federal detention center.

Late Thursday night, in response to a lawsuit brought by Mr. Ragbir's lawyers, a Federal District Court judge in Manhattan granted him a temporary stay of removal and a hearing on Jan. 29 to determine whether the agents were right to detain him.

The judge, Katherine B. Forrest, ordered Mr. Ragbir to be detained in the New York area so that he could be near his lawyer and family. On Friday, the government contested the order. A hearing that will deal with whether he can be brought back from Miami will be held in the District Court of the Southern District of New York on Tuesday.

Mr. Ragbir became an immigrant rights activist because of his own case. He came to the United States in 1991 from Trinidad and Tobago. He had been a lawful permanent resident when he was convicted of wire fraud in 2000. After he served his sentence, Mr. Ragbir was ordered deported in 2006 and detained by immigration officials.

In 2011, the New York field office of ICE granted him a stay of removal. Last April, he was granted an extension of that stay, but only until Jan. 19, eight days after his check-in.

Mr. Ragbir was not the only high-profile immigrant rights leader arrested in a one-week span. On Thursday night, immigration authorities detained Eliseo Jurado, the husband of Ingrid Latorre, who is fighting deportation as she takes sanctuary in a Colorado church.

Last week, a co-founder of New Sanctuary in New York was detained; Jean Montrevil, a native of Haiti, was picked up near his home in Far Rockaway, Queens, two weeks before a scheduled check-in.

"It seems really clear to us that this is an escalation of retaliation, not just against individual rights leaders, but against the right of the movement to exist," said Mary Small, the policy director for Detention Watch Network, an immigrant rights group.

TODD HEISLER/THE NEW YORK TIMES

In early 2018, immigration officials detained Eliseo Jurado, right, the husband of immigrant rights activist Ingrid Latorre, left.

Rachael Yong Yow, a spokeswoman for the New York field office of ICE, said in a statement on Thursday that in the last 12 years Mr. Ragbir's immigration case has undergone extensive judicial review at multiple levels.

"In each review, the courts have uniformly held that Mr. Ragbir does not have a legal basis to remain in the U.S.," she said. "He has since exhausted his petitions and appeals through the immigration courts, the Board of Immigration Appeals, and the U.S. District Court. He will remain in custody pending removal to Trinidad."

Ms. Gottlieb said she understood the legal disagreements over the case, but questioned the government's lack of transparency in its operations.

"Basic human decency requires that his wife and lawyers know where he is, so that we don't live in a country where people are whisked away to secret facilities," Ms. Gottlieb said.

Ms. Yong Yow declined to comment on the pending hearing.

ICE Detained My Husband for Being an Activist

OPINION | BY AMY GOTTLIEB | JAN. 18, 2018

LAST THURSDAY, I found myself in the back of an ambulance with my handcuffed husband, Ravi Ragbir, two E.M.T.s and an agent from Immigration and Customs Enforcement.

As the ambulance inched its way out of 26 Federal Plaza in Manhattan, I caught glimpses of the chaos outside. Faces of friends swam in and out of view. We could hear the shouts and wails of the hundreds of supporters surrounding us who knew Ravi had been arrested, feared he was being "disappeared" and were attempting, nonviolently, with their bodies, to protect him.

Ravi's arrest is the latest in a series that makes clear that ICE is singling out immigrant activists and leaders for detention and deportation. In the past week alone we have learned of three other leaders who have been deported, detained or placed into deportation proceedings. Each of these leaders has been outspoken about his or her own immigration case and has worked toward a more just system for all.

Ravi is an immigrant from Trinidad and the executive director of the New Sanctuary Coalition of New York City, a network of faith groups that works to reform detention and deportation practices. Eighteen years ago, he served time for a wire fraud conviction; after he finished his sentence, ICE detained him. He had been a legal permanent resident, but his green card was taken away, and he has been fighting a deportation order since 2006.

Ravi and I met through our mutual work on immigrant rights and married in 2010. Even though I am an American citizen, Ravi continues to face deportation because of his conviction years ago. As he fights his own deportation, he works with other immigrants in New York, accompanying them to their ICE check-ins, developing a legal support clinic and organizing churches and synagogues to fight deportation.

Last week, Ravi had his regularly scheduled check-in with ICE. Once routine, these check-ins have become terrifying under President Trump, with immigrants being detained and deported after meeting with officials.

When Ravi, his lawyer and I walked into the building, we were more nervous than usual, even though nothing had changed in Ravi's case.

We had reason to fear: A week earlier, ICE agents in unmarked vans detained another immigration leader, Jean Montrevil, as he went home for lunch the day before his check-in. He has been deported to Haiti. On the same day Ravi was detained, ICE detained Eliseo Jurado, an immigrant rights leader in Colorado, and a week later, another leader, Maru Mora-Villalpando, announced that she received a notice to appear in immigration court in Seattle.

When the ICE officer told us that Ravi's legal options were exhausted and that he would be deported, Ravi passed out. I held him tightly and he revived; someone called for medical attention.

By nighttime, Ravi had been flown to Miami. I spent the day unsure where he was and struggling to accept that my husband had been taken from me.

As a longtime immigrant rights lawyer and advocate, I am aware of the horrific conditions in the jails that hold immigrants. I know how deportation tears at the fabric of families and communities.

But now I am inside this nightmare personally and it hurts more than I ever thought it would. I come home to an empty apartment, and everything screams Ravi's absence.

Like Jean and thousands of other immigrants caught in ICE raids, Ravi threatens no one. On the contrary, he and other immigrant leaders have led their communities with dignity and courage in a brutal time. That's why they were snatched — and why ICE wants to deport them.

The last time I saw my husband was through Plexiglas at the Krome Detention Center in Miami. After six tense days and a court hearing on Tuesday, ICE said it would bring Ravi back to the New York area so that he could be closer to his family, his legal counsel and his community. But he remains detained, and he is still not safe from deportation.

We are continuing to challenge his detention. My greatest fear is that he will be sent back to Trinidad, where he has not lived for more than 25 years. We must keep Ravi, and other immigrant leaders, at home in the United States where they belong.

AMY GOTTLIEB IS THE ASSOCIATE REGIONAL DIRECTOR OF THE AMERICAN FRIENDS SERVICE COMMITTEE.

President Trump, How Is This Man a Danger?

OPINION | BY NICHOLAS KRISTOF | FEB. 10, 2018

PRESIDENT TRUMP suggests that the aim of his crackdown on immigrants is to "defend Americans" from "savage," "worst of the worst" intruders who kill Americans or at least are "dangerous criminals."

What does Trump's crackdown look like in real life? In Lawrence, Kan., the other day, immigration agents handcuffed a beloved chemistry professor as he was leaving his home to drive his daughter to school. Then they warned his crying wife and children, ages 7 to 14, that they could be arrested if they tried to hug him goodbye, and drove off with him — leaving a shattered family behind.

"I'm a normal 12-year-old with a dad like everybody else's dad," the daughter he was about to drive that morning, Naheen Jamal, told me. "I don't understand why this is happening."

Her dad, Syed A. Jamal, 55, had been in America for 30 years, having arrived legally from Bangladesh as a student, before overstaying his visa. He loved Kansas and settled in Lawrence, teaching at local colleges and volunteering at local schools — even running for the school board. He coached students in science and sports.

> But President Trump, you say that these people are "criminals, drug dealers, rapists" and that we must be protected from them.

Jamal, who seems just about the least dangerous person in America, is now in jail pending deportation to Bangladesh. A court intervened with a temporary stay as the government was trying to rush him out of the country.

While this arrest has done nothing to make anyone safer, it is devastating for three American citizens in particular — his children. Their mom, Angela, also of Bangladeshi origin, donated a kidney last year, and Jamal is the only source of family income.

If Jamal is indeed deported, his family will be upended. Randy Capps of the Migration Policy Institute estimates that 25,000 people deported in 2016 have children who are American citizens.

Researchers have found that such children often bounce around among relatives, suffer in school and display self-destructive behaviors, such as cutting themselves.

"It's insane," said Marci Leuschen, a high school biology teacher and friend of the Jamal family who has helped organize a campaign in Lawrence to support the family. Some 500 people showed up at a local church to write letters in support of Jamal, and Leuschen said some were Trump supporters who were aghast that the immigration crackdown meant locking up their friend.

On Change.org, more than 66,000 have signed a petition calling for Jamal to be freed. A GoFundMe campaign has raised more than $39,000 for legal and other expenses.

> *Thank you, President Trump, for defending us from such "bad hombres" — even if Professor Jamal hasn't been accused of any violence, in contrast to your (recently ousted) staff secretary.*

Naheen said that the outpouring of community support has overwhelmed her. "It's what keeps me going," she told me. "Everyone in my community, I feel so grateful to them."

Jamal earned a graduate degree in pharmaceutical sciences, worked as a researcher in cancer and genetics and became renowned for helping others. He even assisted elderly neighbors with their weekly shopping and checked on their medicines.

"The truth is, the country needs more neighbors like Syed," wrote a local pastor, Eleanor McCormick, whose Plymouth Congregational Church in Lawrence has helped lead the grass-roots effort to support him.

Jamal has had a tortuous series of interactions with the impossibly complex immigration system. Several years ago, immigration authorities ruled that he had overstayed his visa, but the Obama administration exercised discretion, and (like countless others) he was allowed to stay if he reported in regularly. So Jamal had a temporary work permit and checked in with the immigration authorities, most recently on Jan. 7. Everything seemed to be fine — until the immigration officers decided for some reason to blow up his family's life.

> *Thank you, Mr. President, for shielding us from the "worst of the worst" chemistry professors.*

Carl Rusnok, a spokesman for Immigration and Customs Enforcement, did not try to argue that Jamal is a threat. He said that the priority is to arrest criminals (as it was under Barack Obama) but that no one is excluded.

The American immigration system is a mess, and I don't pretend there are easy solutions. But I don't think we should lightly deport people who may have violated immigration rules but pose no threat and are embedded in American society — people like, well, Melania Trump, who worked without authorization on her visitor visa when she first came to the U.S., according to an investigation by The Associated Press.

I do believe it's important to hold individuals to account for misconduct. So I tried to ask Homeland Security Secretary Kirstjen Nielsen why she is determined to destroy the lives of the Americans in the Jamal family. She did not respond, perhaps because she was too busy being a good citizen helping elderly neighbors with their groceries. Or maybe just deporting "savage" immigrants to protect Americans.

CHAPTER 5

The Politics of Immigration

While the experience of relocating to a new country is personal to every immigrant, politicians view the process on a public scale. One of the many roles of the U.S. government is to ensure that immigration does not have a negative effect on American citizens. The Department of Homeland Security attempts to strike a balance between protecting their current constituents and supporting new and potential residents of the United States. Some methods it has employed to manage immigration include quotas, security checks, travel bans, legal action and deportation.

Court Ruling May Open Way for More Political Refugees

BY ROBERT PEAR | MARCH 15, 1987

THE SUPREME COURT decides relatively few cases involving immigration, and in even fewer does it uphold the rights of aliens. But last week, aliens won a big victory as the High Court ruled that the Government must relax its standard for deciding if they are eligible for asylum.

Asylum, defined as a place of refuge, shelter or protection, is what thousands of people fleeing persecution seek in the United States. Under the Refugee Act of 1980, aliens may qualify if they have "a well-founded fear of persecution" in their homeland "on account of race, religion, nationality, membership in a particular social group, or political opinion." Prior law, reflecting Cold War attitudes, explicitly favored refugees from Communist countries. The 1980 law was intended to eliminate ideological restrictions.

There has been a furious debate about whether the Reagan Administration has applied the standard in an evenhanded manner. Critics on the left and the right say the Administration tailors its decisions on asylum to fit foreign policy goals or ideological preconceptions. Liberals say the Immigration and Naturalization Service has looked unfavorably on applications from Salvadorans because El Salvador is an ally. Conservatives complain bitterly about rejections of Poles and other Eastern Europeans.

Even as President Reagan has denounced the Sandinista Government, the immigration service has rejected thousands of Nicaraguans, saying they could not show that they would be singled out for persecution at home. The Supreme Court decision involved a 38-year-old Nicaraguan who said she faced torture because of her brother's political activities. The Administration had argued that aliens must demonstrate "a clear probability of persecution" to qualify for asylum. But the Court, in a 6-to-3 decision, said the "plain language" of the 1980 law indicated that Congress had established a "more generous" standard.

An alien may be eligible for asylum if he can show that "persecution is a reasonable possibility," Associate Justice John Paul Stevens suggested in the majority opinion. A person with "a 10 percent chance of being shot, tortured or otherwise persecuted" might qualify, he added. Since the statutory test is "a well-founded fear of persecution," the alien's "subjective mental state" is a key factor, Justice Stevens said, but the standard will be given "concrete meaning" only as the Government rules on individual cases.

Gilbert Paul Carrasco, associate director of migration and refugee services for the United States Catholic Conference, said it will now be "easier for aliens to prove their eligibility for asylum." He predicted increases in applications for asylum and in numbers approved, because "the Court has sent a clear message." Paul W. Schmidt, acting general counsel of the immigration service, said thousands of people, "virtually everybody who has had asylum denied and is still in this country, will file a motion to have his or her case reopened and reconsidered under the new standard." But Verne Jervis, an immigration service spokesman, predicted that most aliens still will not qualify because they cannot show a well-founded fear of persecution.

A recent study for Congress by the General Accounting Office said that only 2 percent of aliens denied asylum were actually deported from the United States. Some are waiting for hearings before immigration judges, and many are in an "uncertain status"; there was no evidence they had left the country. The immigration service does not have the money or personnel to locate and deport them. The Government received 18,889 applications for asylum last year, granted 3,359 and denied 7,882. Some are pending. The G.A.O. found a much higher approval rate for some countries, such as Iran and Poland, than for others, such as El Salvador and Nicaragua. The Government, it noted, "generally does not document the reasons why applications are approved or denied."

While approval rates may rise as a result of the Supreme Court decision, aliens fearing persecution will still not have an absolute right to asylum. For, as the Court said, "the Attorney General is not required to grant asylum to everyone" who passes the statutory test for eligibility. Under the 1980 law, the decision is subject to "the discretion of the Attorney General." Mr. Schmidt said people who met the standard could be rejected if, for example, they used fraudulent documents to get to this country.

Wade J. Henderson of the American Civil Liberties Union said that "from a symbolic point of view, the decision is a significant victory for human rights advocates, civil libertarians and workers in the sanctuary movement," who assist migrants from Central America. "In practical terms, it will not be a panacea because the Attorney General retains discretion to decide when asylum should be granted." He urged Congress to pass legislation temporarily suspending the deportation of Salvadorans and Nicaraguans while the G.A.O. studies conditions in their countries. Senator Dennis DeConcini of Arizona and Representative Joe Moakley of Massachusetts, both Democrats, have championed such legislation. The Administration strongly opposes it, contending that many of the intended beneficiaries are not victims of persecution but "economic migrants" seeking a better life.

New Alliances and Attitudes on Aid

BY CELIA W. DUGGER | AUG. 1, 1997

THE DECISION by the President and Congress to restore benefits to half a million elderly and disabled legal immigrants in Tuesday's budget agreement provides a window on the volatile politics of immigration and the way legislators' attitudes toward immigrants can swing from suspicion to sympathy.

Last summer, Republican Congressional leaders depicted many immigrants as people from the Third World whose families were abusing the generosity of the United States so their old folks could live off the taxpayers. Now, prominent Republicans who supported the cutoff last summer — including Senator Alfonse M. D'Amato of New York — are emphasizing protection of innocent, aged people from destitution.

"You know, Republicans have a heart, too," said Representative E. Clay Shaw Jr., a South Florida Republican who was instrumental in cutting off Supplemental Security Income, or S.S.I., to legal immigrants last year, but who said yesterday that he had worried about the consequences for the elderly who depended on them.

A strange-bedfellows alliance was crucial to restoring the benefits, estimated to cost $11.4 billion over five years. Mayor Rudolph W. Giuliani was at the head of the lobbying line of governors and mayors, some of them Republicans from high-immigration states, who were convinced that immigrants who lost their Federal benefits would become a fiscal burden on state and local governments.

Joining them were advocates for immigrants who collected sad stories about individual cases of hardship that appeared in newspapers across the country.

"That created outrage and made what happened real in the way that months of advocacy before the bill passed failed to do," said Cecilia Munoz, deputy vice president for policy at the National Council of La Raza, a nonprofit Hispanic civil rights group in Washington.

And President Clinton, who made restoring the benefits a priority in budget negotiations, provided the leverage to shift the position of Congressional Republicans who had pushed last year for the provisions, with some support from Democrats. Advocates for immigrants were horrified last year when the President signed the 1996 welfare bill on Aug. 22, despite his own opposition to provisions that denied benefits to legal immigrants already in the country.

"In less than a year since they shredded the safety net for legal immigrants, Congress and the President have decided to restore much of it," said Frank Sharry, executive director of the National Immigration Forum, an advocacy group in Washington. "That's a remarkable political turnaround."

But the budget agreement does not restore everything that legal immigrants lost in the welfare bill. Those who arrive in the United States after Aug. 22, 1996 and subsequently become aged or disabled will still be ineligible for S.S.I., which provides monthly cash payments to poor people who are aged or disabled.

And a million legal immigrants who are not citizens will still lose food stamp benefits by the end of August, Federal officials estimate.

Advocates who had pushed to restore S.S.I. benefits say they will now turn their attention to food stamps. A study commissioned by the Department of Agriculture, which operates the food stamp program, estimates that about 1 in 6 of the immigrant food stamp recipients are children and another 1 in 6 are elderly. Almost one-third of the immigrant recipients are working poor.

Whatever the outcome of the next skirmish on benefits, the landscape of American politics has come to seem a much less hospitable place to legal immigrants since Congress voted last year to cut off S.S.I. and food stamps to most of them.

"There used to be a bargain between immigrants and the United States," said Demetrios G. Papademetriou, director of the international migration program at the Carnegie Endowment for International Peace. "That bargain was that you came here, worked hard and we created a level playing field. We didn't treat you differently. We undid that bargain last year."

Immigrants' fears about losing access to the United States' social safety net have helped to propel hundreds of thousands of them to seek citizenship, a rush that is expected to produce 1.8 million naturalization applications this year.

The effort to deny benefits to legal immigrants, and the harsh tone of much of last year's debate on immigration issues, have not only mobilized legal immigrants to become citizens, but some Republicans and immigration experts say they also may politicize the new citizens and their American-born citizen children, boomeranging on Republicans.

In the 1996 Presidential election, surveys at the polls found that Mr. Clinton had improved his showing among Hispanic voters since the previous election, to 72 percent from 61 percent, and among Asians, to 43 percent from 31 percent. The Republican Presidential candidate, Bob Dole, received 21 percent of the Hispanic vote, down from the 25 percent received in 1992 by George Bush. Mr. Dole got 48 percent of the Asian-American vote, down from Mr. Bush's 55 percent.

"The message was clear to immigrant communities: 'Hey, the Republican Party is giving us every indication they don't want us in their big tent,' " said Representative Ileana Ros-Lehtinen, a naturalized, Cuban-born Republican from Florida. "We took a hit in the last Presidential election, no doubt about it."

Mrs. Ros-Lehtinen lobbied within her party for the restoration of benefits and hopes it will heal some political wounds.

It is hard to measure how much the flip-flop on S.S.I. was based on political calculation as opposed to a substantive reconsideration of the issue. Some in Congress said they did not realize how harsh the effects of the cutoff of benefits would be until after they voted for the measure.

Senator Mike DeWine, Republican of Ohio, said he had thought that legal immigrants who really needed help would become citizens to requalify. Only later, he said, did he realize that many could not naturalize, either because they were mentally incompetent to take the oath or too old to learn enough English to pass the citizenship test.

"It seemed wrong to change the rules for them," Mr. DeWine said, explaining his own change of heart.

Mr. D'Amato said he decided too many old, ailing people would be left with no means of financial support.

The willingness of influential members of Congress to soften their stance on benefits for vulnerable immigrants may also reflect a broad national indifference to the issue of immigration. That apathy, combined with the passionate interest of immigrants and their advocates, may have given Congress the political room to change its collective mind.

When asked directly by pollsters whether there should be more or less immigration to the United States, a majority of Americans have replied in the 1990's that immigration levels should be reduced. But when asked generally what is the most important issue facing the country, less than 1 percent name immigration.

"Consistently, in poll after poll, immigration ranks lower than 'don't know,' " said Thomas J. Espenshade, a sociology professor at Princeton University. "I don't think it's really a voting issue, except maybe in some very high immigration pockets."

So perhaps it is not surprising that in the last year, Republican-led efforts to sharply reduce legal immigration and to deny public education to the children of illegal immigrants were both defeated in Congress.

Alan Brinkley, a history professor at Columbia University, said the moment reminds him of the late 19th century. "There are a lot of people who feel vaguely that too many immigrants are coming, but the anti-immigrant sentiment is not yet strong enough to dominate the discourse," he said.

U.S. Will Seek to Fingerprint Visas' Holders

BY ERIC SCHMITT | JUNE 5, 2002

THE JUSTICE DEPARTMENT will propose new regulations this week requiring tens of thousands of Muslim and Middle Eastern visa holders to register with the government and be fingerprinted, administration officials said today.

The initiative, the subject of intense debate within the administration, is designed for "individuals from countries who pose the highest risk to our security," including most visa holders from Saudi Arabia, Pakistan and many other Muslim nations, officials said. More than 100,000 foreigners, including students, workers, researchers and tourists, all foreigners from designated countries who do not hold green cards, would probably be covered by the plan, an official said.

Antiterrorism teams made up of federal, state and local officers that have been formed in most larger cities since the Sept. 11 attacks would help immigration officials register visa holders already living here, using procedures similar to those employed to find 5,000 mainly Middle Eastern men who were sought for interviews after the attacks.

New arrivals from the designated countries would be fingerprinted at airports or seaports and be required to register with the Immigration and Naturalization Service after 30 days in the country, officials said.

Violators could be fined, refused re-entry into the United States or possibly deported, officials said.

The plan will be published in the Federal Register. After a comment period, it will become a Justice Department regulation.

The proposal ignited a raging debate in the Bush administration. White House officials supported the Justice proposal, but the State Department lodged objections, fearing diplomatic repercussions with allies in the war on terror, administration officials said.

A Justice Department spokeswoman, Susan Dryden, declined to comment on the proposal.

Immigration specialists, meantime, are warning of new backlogs at airports if already understaffed immigration service inspectors are required to fingerprint and process a new category of visitors.

But some civil liberties and Arab-American groups expressed outrage at the proposed requirements, arguing that such a policy was a blatant example of racial and ethnic profiling.

"What's the logic of this?" said Jeanne Butterfield, executive director of the American Immigration Lawyers Association. "Anyone who's truly dangerous is not going to show up to be registered."

James J. Zogby, president of the Arab American Institute, a policy organization, said the registration plan would be "an overtly discriminatory, inefficient and ineffective way to deal with the problem."

"This is targeting a group of people, the overwhelming majority of whom are innocent, but whose lives will be turned upside down," Mr. Zogby added. "The message it sends is that we're becoming like the Soviet Union, with people registering at police stations."

The authority for proposing the new registration requirements rests in a long-dormant provision in the Immigration and Nationality Act of 1952, administration officials said.

A section of that law requires all foreign visa holders to register with the government if they remain in the United States for 30 days or longer. The law also required the fingerprinting of virtually all foreigners who were not permanent residents, except for diplomats.

The law remained on the books, but enforcement fell off in the early 1980's when the volume of visa holders climbed rapidly and the immigration service's budget and staffing dropped.

"By the early 1980's, the sheer volume of the effort combined with a lack of funding resulted in the practice being discontinued," said one administration official.

In 1979, the same year as the beginning of the Iranian hostage crisis, Iranian students were required to register with the government.

After the attacks last year, most visa holders from Iran, Iraq, Sudan and Libya were fingerprinted as they entered the United States.

But the terrorist attacks had given fresh impetus to a much broader program. One administration official said the new registration proposal, which Justice officials planned to brief to Congress on Wednesday and announce later this week, would give the government a leg up on identifying the highest-risk foreign visitors now living in the United States.

Congress has required that the Immigration and Naturalization Service establish a system to monitor the entry and departure of all immigrants, beginning in 2003.

But other officials said the contentious proposal broke free from an internal administration debate only amid the recent recriminations over what intelligence the Federal Bureau of Investigation, Central Intelligence Agency and other federal agencies possessed before Sept. 11 about the possibilities of a terrorist attack.

One of the leaders of the interagency discussion on the alien registration proposal is a conservative University of Missouri at Kansas City law professor, Kris W. Kobach, officials said.

Although Mr. Kobach, 36, is only a White House fellow on temporary assignment to the Justice Department, he also played a central role in another contentious proposal to give state and local police departments the power to track down illegal immigrants as a new tactic in the global war on terror.

New Policy Delays Visas for Specified Muslim Men

BY RAYMOND BONNER | SEPT. 10, 2002

UNDER A POLICY quietly imposed by the Bush administration three months ago, tens of thousands of Muslim men, from more than 26 countries, have not been able to get United States visas, disrupting lives, creating diplomatic tensions and causing headaches for American diplomats.

The policy requires that officials in Washington approve visas for every male between the ages of 16 and 45 who is a native of any one of 26 countries. Most are in the Mideast, but the list also includes Pakistan, Malaysia and Indonesia, several diplomats said.

Even if a man does not live in one of those countries, but he or a close relative was born in one of them, his visa application must be sent for approval. Before Sept. 11, consular offices or embassies could issue most visas after a routine check.

After Sept. 11, applications from men in this category had to be sent to Washington, and if nothing negative turned up in 30 days, the embassy could issue the visa. Now the consular office must send the application to Washington and wait for a response. The policy was changed because the administration found that there were too many applications to review adequately within 30 days, diplomats said.

The delays now are interminable. One American official said there was a backlog of least 100,000 visa applications, now being reviewed by the F.B.I. and C.I.A.

At a time that the United States is trying to improve its image and win friends, American diplomats say the policy is generating widespread hostility in the very countries and population — Muslim men — from which the Bush administration most wants to gain support.

The visa applicants are primarily university students, many of whom had gone home for the summer vacation and are now unable to resume their studies, and business executives with American companies, who want to travel to the United States for sales conferences and other meetings at their headquarters, American diplomats said.

In Indonesia, a country crippled by corruption, there was widespread support for a program to send 54 civil servants to Los Angeles last month for a seminar about stemming corruption, followed by visits to offices in Washington and New York that dealt with the issue. But 51 of the individuals were unable to get their visas, the program's organizers said; of the 3 who did, one is a woman and the other two are men over 50.

"There are so many horror stories in the region," said a senior American diplomat in the Middle East. "We say we need to improve our image," he went on. "To do that people need to understand us. To do that we need more exchange programs." The men being denied visas and thus access to these programs, he said, "are the very people we want to engage, want to influence."

American officials say they cannot tell an applicant how long it will take for word from Washington, and that very few visas have been issued to men in this category.

In Singapore, it took a call from a cabinet minister to the American ambassador, Franklin L. Lavin, to get a visa for someone who had a scholarship to Stanford.

"It's been 22 years since I did consular work," Mr. Lavin said, laughing. But he added more seriously, "Don't we want to encourage more of these guys to get degrees in the U.S.?"

Singapore is not on the list of countries that automatically attract scrutiny, but many Singaporean residents were born in one of the suspect countries, or an immediate relative was, and that makes them subject to the policy. Several hundred students from Singapore are waiting for their visas in order to start school in the United States, Mr. Lavin said.

"It's certainly not creating good will," he added.

In Malaysia, also, several hundred students who have been admitted to American universities, usually with scholarships, have been unable to get to the United States for classes, said Donald McCloud, director of the Malaysian-American Commission on Educational Exchange. The State Department-funded organization administers the Fulbright program and encourages Malaysian students to go to the United States for study.

He said a majority of the applicants were ethnic Chinese and are not even Muslims. "They are certainly not terrorist material at all, but they're getting nailed."

In Indonesia, at least 400 students are stranded, unable to go to the United States for the start of this school year, officials said.

One of them, Anies, is a doctoral student in political science at Northern Illinois University who had come home to do some research. He had studied on a Fulbright at the University of Maryland and had received a master's degree.

On July 15, he went to the embassy to apply for renewal of his visa and was interviewed by a consular officer. He was told to return in a month to pick up his visa. But when he went back on Aug. 16, it was not ready. "I'm still waiting," he said.

There is now a backlog of 2,500 visa applicants here, most from businessmen, embassy officials said.

Like Anies, they can check a Web site the embassy here set up to advise them on what is happening (usembassyjakarta.org/pickup.html). Every day, like today, the message is the same, Anies said: "There are no visas ready to be picked up at this time."

Republican Split on Immigration Reflects Nation's Struggle

BY RACHEL L. SWARNS | MARCH 29, 2006

WASHINGTON, MARCH 28 — It is almost as if they are looking at two different Americas.

The Senate Republicans who voted on Monday to legalize the nation's illegal immigrants look at the waves of immigration reshaping this country and see a powerful work force, millions of potential voters and future Americans.

The House Republicans who backed tough border security legislation in December look at the same group of people and see a flood of invaders and lawbreakers who threaten national security and American jobs and culture.

But both wings of the deeply divided Republican Party are responding to the same phenomenon: the demographic shift driven by immigration in recent decades, a wave that is quietly transforming small towns and cities across the country and underscoring pressures on many parts of the economy.

The United States has always been a nation of immigrants, but today the country has more than 33 million foreign-born residents, the largest number since the Census started keeping such statistics in 1850. In 2003, foreign-born residents made up 11.7 percent of the population, the highest percentage since 1910. And over the past 16 years, the newcomers, many of them illegal, have poured into places in the South and Midwest that have not seen sizeable numbers of new immigrants in generations.

The question of how to cope with the 11 million illegal immigrants believed to be living here — whether to integrate them, ignore them or try to send them home somehow — is a question gripping many ordinary citizens, religious leaders, state legislators and policy makers in the White House. And in their bitter, fractious debate, Republicans in

Congress are reflecting what some describe as the nation's struggle to define itself and, to some degree, politically align itself, during a period of social change.

The Senate Republicans on the Judiciary Committee who emerged victorious on Monday with help from Democrats argue that those illegal immigrants who work, pay taxes and learn English should be fully incorporated into American society as citizens. The House Republicans who passed a far different bill in December are pushing to criminalize their presence in the United States. (The full Senate is expected to vote on immigration legislation next week. Any bill that passes the Senate will have to be reconciled with the House legislation.)

As the party struggles to reconcile these competing visions, frustrations over the stalemate are spilling onto the airwaves and into the streets as some conservatives on talk radio call for a wall to be built along the Mexican border and tens of thousands of immigrants and their supporters march in favor of citizenship.

"Right now, we're seeing to some extent the political response to the demography," said Roberto Suro, executive director of the Pew Hispanic Center, a nonpartisan research group in Washington. "And even though the legislative proposals are seemingly technical and narrow, they touch these nerves about how we think of ourselves as a people."

"You end up, after a point, trying to balance our fundamental traditions, the need for order, law and security with a need for openness," he said. "Immigration policy, writ large, has always been partly a matter of national identity. It becomes a values-laden debate. Congress has a hard time with it."

That difficulty reflects, in part, the swiftness and the enormousness of the demographic shift.

In 1970, there were 9.6 million foreign-born residents in the country, census data show. By 1980, that figure had surged to 14.1 million. Between 1990 and 2000, the number of foreign-born residents jumped to 31.1 million from 19.8 million.

Senator Sam Brownback, Republican of Kansas, who voted for the legalization of illegal immigrants on Monday, says he has seen and felt the shift in his own state.

"Huge increase," he said of the number of new immigrants. "It's a big issue, and it's one where communities that have adapted to it are more accepting and others are more questioning about the scale of what's taking place."

But when he wrestled with the issue, Mr. Brownback decided that he could not join the ranks of those who wanted simply to push out illegal immigrants. "This is also about the hallmark of a compassionate society, what you do with the widows, the orphans and the foreigners among you," he said.

Senator Lindsey Graham, Republican of South Carolina, echoed those thoughts in his defense of the legalization program, which would ultimately grant immigrants citizenship.

"Where is home?" Mr. Graham asked his colleagues Monday. "Their home is where they've raised their children. Their home is where they've lived their married lives."

"Whatever we do," he added, "we have to recognize that for several generations people have made America their home."

But to Representative Tom Tancredo, the Colorado Republican who helped spearhead the border security bill in the House, illegal immigrants are far from welcome or essential to this country.

He was not moved when he saw the tens of thousands of immigrants, some illegal, and their supporters rallying against his bill. He said he was outraged that people he viewed as lawbreakers felt comfortable enough to stand without fear in front of the television cameras.

"For years, the government has turned a blind eye to illegal immigrants who break into this country," Mr. Tancredo said. "It isn't any wonder that illegal aliens now act as if they are entitled to the rights and privileges of citizenship."

Mr. Tancredo's view of the illegal immigrant as an unwanted outsider, an encroacher, is far from uncommon.

strengthened our country in so many ways. These are not contradictory goals. America can be a lawful society and a welcoming society at the same time. We will fix the problems created by illegal immigration, and we will deliver a system that is secure, orderly and fair.

So I support comprehensive immigration reform that will accomplish five clear objectives.

SECURING THE BORDERS

First, the United States must secure its borders. This is a basic responsibility of a sovereign nation. It is also an urgent requirement of our national security. Our objective is straightforward: The border should be open to trade and lawful immigration and shut to illegal immigrants, as well as criminals, drug dealers and terrorists.

I was the governor of a state that has a 1,200-mile border with Mexico. So I know how difficult it is to enforce the border and how important it is. Since I became president, we've increased funding for border security by 66 percent and expanded the Border Patrol from about 9,000 to 12,000 agents. The men and women of our Border Patrol are doing a fine job in difficult circumstances, and over the past five years they have apprehended and sent home about six million people entering America illegally.

Despite this progress, we do not yet have full control of the border, and I am determined to change that. Tonight I'm calling on Congress to provide funding for dramatic improvements in manpower and technology at the border. By the end of 2008, we will increase the number of Border Patrol officers by an additional 6,000. When these new agents are deployed, we will have more than doubled the size of the Border Patrol during my presidency.

At the same time, we are launching the most technologically advanced border security initiative in American history. We will construct high-tech fences in urban corridors and build new patrol roads and barriers in rural areas. We will employ motion sensors, infrared cameras and unmanned aerial vehicles to prevent illegal crossings.

America has the best technology in the world, and we will ensure that the Border Patrol has the technology they need to do their job and secure our border.

Training thousands of new Border Patrol agents and bringing the most advanced technology to the border will take time. Yet the need to secure our border is urgent. So I'm announcing several immediate steps to strengthen border enforcement during this period of transition.

One way to help during this transition is to use the National Guard. So in coordination with governors, up to 6,000 Guard members will be deployed to our southern border. The Border Patrol will remain in the lead. The Guard will assist the Border Patrol by operating surveillance systems, analyzing intelligence, installing fences and vehicle barriers, building patrol roads and providing training. Guard units will not be involved in direct law enforcement activities. That duty will be done by the Border Patrol.

This initial commitment of Guard members would last for a period of one year. After that, the number of Guard forces will be reduced as new Border Patrol agents and new technologies come online. It is important for Americans to know that we have enough Guard forces to win the war on terror, to respond to natural disasters and help secure our border.

The United States is not going to militarize the southern border. Mexico is our neighbor and our friend. We will continue to work cooperatively to improve security on both sides of the border, to confront common problems like drug trafficking and crime and to reduce illegal immigration.

Another way to help during this period of transition is through state and local law enforcement in our border communities. So we will increase federal funding for state and local authorities assisting the Border Patrol on targeted enforcement missions. We will give state and local authorities the specialized training they need to help federal officers apprehend and detain illegal immigrants. State and local law enforcement officials are an important part of our border security and they need to be a part of our strategy to secure our borders.

The steps I have outlined will improve our ability to catch people entering our country illegally. At the same time, we must ensure that every illegal immigrant we catch crossing our southern border is returned home. More than 85 percent of the illegal immigrants we catch crossing the southern border are Mexicans, and most are sent back home within 24 hours.

But when we catch illegal immigrants from other countries, it is not as easy to send them back home. For many years, the government did not have enough space in our detention facilities to hold them while the legal process unfolded. So most were released back into our society and asked to return for a court date. When the date arrived, the vast majority did not show up. This practice, called catch and release, is unacceptable, and we will end it.

TEMPORARY WORKER PROGRAM

Second, to secure our border, we must create a temporary worker program. The reality is that there are many people on the other side of our border who will do anything to come to America to work and build a better life. They walk across miles of desert in the summer heat or hide in the back of 18-wheelers to reach our country. This creates enormous pressure on our border that walls and patrols alone will not stop. To secure the border effectively, we must reduce the numbers of people trying to sneak across.

Therefore, I support a temporary worker program that would create a legal path for foreign workers to enter our country in an orderly way, for a limited period of time. This program would match willing foreign workers with willing American employers for jobs Americans are not doing. Every worker who applies for the program would be required to pass criminal background checks. And temporary workers must return to their home country at the conclusion of their stay.

A temporary worker program would meet the needs of our economy, and it would give honest immigrants a way to provide for their families while respecting the law. A temporary worker program would reduce the appeal of human smugglers and make it less likely that people would risk their lives to cross the border. It would ease the financial burden on state and local governments by replacing illegal workers with lawful taxpayers. And above all, a temporary worker program would add to our security by making certain we know who is in our country and why they are here.

IDENTIFICATION CARDS

Third, we need to hold employers to account for the workers they hire. It is against the law to hire someone who is in this country illegally. Yet businesses often cannot verify the legal status of their employees because of the widespread problem of document fraud. Therefore, comprehensive immigration reform must include a better system for verifying documents and work eligibility.

A key part of that system should be a new identification card for every legal foreign worker. This card should use biometric technology, such as digital fingerprints, to make it tamperproof. A tamperproof card would help us enforce the law and leave employers with no excuse for violating it. And by making it harder for illegal immigrants to find work in our country, we would discourage people from crossing the border illegally in the first place.

CITIZENSHIP AND DEPORTATION

Fourth, we must face the reality that millions of illegal immigrants are here already. They should not be given an automatic path to citizenship. This is amnesty, and I oppose it. Amnesty would be unfair to those who are here lawfully, and it would invite further waves of illegal immigration.

Some in this country argue that the solution is to deport every illegal immigrant and that any proposal short of this amounts to amnesty. I disagree. It is neither wise nor realistic to round up millions of people, many with deep roots in the United States, and send them across the border.

There is a rational middle ground between granting an automatic path to citizenship for every illegal immigrant and a program of mass deportation. That middle ground recognizes there are differences between an illegal immigrant who crossed the border recently and someone who has worked here for many years and has a home, a family and an otherwise clean record.

I believe that illegal immigrants who have roots in our country and want to stay should have to pay a meaningful penalty for breaking the law, to pay their taxes, to learn English and to work in a job for a number of years. People who meet these conditions should be able to apply for citizenship, but approval would not be automatic, and they will have to wait in line behind those who played by the rules and followed the law.

What I've just described is not amnesty; it is a way for those who have broken the law to pay their debt to society and demonstrate the character that makes a good citizen.

SPEAKING ENGLISH

Fifth, we must honor the great American tradition of the melting pot, which has made us one nation out of many peoples. The success of our country depends upon helping newcomers assimilate into our society and embrace our common identity as Americans.

Americans are bound together by our shared ideals, an appreciation of our history, respect for the flag we fly, and an ability to speak and write the English language. English is also the key to unlocking the opportunity of America. English allows newcomers to go from picking crops to opening a grocery, from cleaning offices to running offices, from a life of low-paying jobs to a diploma, a career and a home of their own.

'08 Candidates Weighing Consequences as They Take Sides on Immigration Plan

BY MARC SANTORA | MAY 19, 2007

THE BIPARTISAN IMMIGRATION proposal being taken up by Congress is putting pressure on the leading presidential candidates to take a position on the issue, which could set them up for confrontations with influential constituencies within the two parties.

After the announcement of the bipartisan plan on Thursday, Senator Hillary Rodham Clinton, the New York Democrat, and Rudolph W. Giuliani, the former New York mayor who is one of the Republican frontrunners, were initially noncommittal. Both suggested on Friday that they were open to supporting it, but only with major revisions to some of its main components.

Reflecting the complexity of the issue and the political caution surrounding it, neither of them matched the embrace of the legislation on Thursday by Senator John McCain, the Arizona Republican.

Mr. McCain already faces a direct clash with another of the Republican candidates, Mitt Romney of Massachusetts, who has come out against the bill as he intensifies his efforts to win the support of conservatives who are wary of Mr. McCain and Mr. Giuliani. Mr. Romney's opponents said his position had shifted from more moderate views that he voiced a few years ago.

On Friday, the Romney campaign unveiled a television commercial about illegal immigration that it said would run starting this weekend in New Hampshire and Iowa.

Mr. McCain's position was also assailed on Friday by conservative commentators, who object in particular to the provisions of the legislation that could ultimately grant legal status to many of the estimated 12 million immigrants who are in the United States illegally.

Mr. Giuliani's emphasis has been on whether the legislation would adequately protect the nation from terrorists who might enter the United States illegally.

In an appearance on Friday in Orlando, Fla., he supported the idea of compromise as long as it included a system for registering the people who are currently in America illegally and issuing them identification cards.

"I think this idea of working things out between the Democrats and the Republicans — and each side has to make some compromises in order to get there — then I can see a lot of flexibility there to get that accomplished," he said.

Mrs. Clinton, an aide in her Senate office said, will focus on the provision that would de-emphasize family ties in granting visas, an element of the bill that has drawn fierce objections from many groups and elected officials representing Hispanics.

Mrs. Clinton will try to limit the impact on Hispanic immigrants by offering an amendment to reunite lawful permanent residents with their spouses and minor children by exempting those family members from the visa cap in the bill, the aide said.

When Mrs. Clinton was asked about the bill in New Orleans on Friday, however, she avoided stating any precise position and instead highlighted her support for both toughening border security and providing a path to citizenship for illegal immigrants.

Democrats face a complicated nest of competing interests, including the outcry of some labor unions about the proposed guest worker program and concerns among Hispanic voters that the legislation will severely curtail the ability of families in poorer Latin American countries to settle legally in the United States.

Major labor unions are split on the issue, but there is widespread labor concern about the provision that would set up a temporary guest worker system with no chance of citizenship.

Not only could those workers take away jobs from Americans, these opponents said, but they could also become a permanent underclass.

"The proposal unveiled today includes a massive guest worker program that would allow employers to import hundreds of thousands" of temporary workers every year to perform permanent jobs throughout the economy, John J. Sweeney, president of the AFL-CIO, said in a statement.

John Edwards, the former senator from North Carolina whose campaign has focused on trying to rally traditional union workers with a populist message, said he was pleased to see movement on immigration reform. But, in a statement, Mr. Edwards added, "I have some real concerns about parts of this bill, including the poorly conceived guest worker program."

Senator Barack Obama, Democrat of Illinois, was similarly cautious.

"Without modifications, the proposed bill could devalue the importance of family reunification, replace the current group of undocumented immigrants with a new undocumented population consisting of guest workers who will overstay their visas, and potentially drive down wages of American workers," Mr. Obama said in a statement.

Democrats and Republicans must calculate how their choices will affect them politically, not just in early states like Iowa but also in states like New York, Florida, California and Texas that have large immigrant populations.

Muzaffar Chishti, the director of the Migration Policy Institute's office at the New York University law school, said that the pressure was going to quickly build for everyone to declare firm positions.

"Next week is going to be very, very critical," Mr. Chishti said. "The pressure on the senators between now and Monday is going to be intense."

MICHAEL COOPER, STEVEN GREENHOUSE, PATRICK HEALY AND MICHAEL LUO CONTRIBUTED REPORTING.

CHAPTER 6

Immigration and President Donald J. Trump

President Trump's strong views on immigration were a focal point during his 2016 presidential campaign. Among his campaign policies were promises to deport millions of illegal immigrants, ban Muslims from entering the country and build a wall on the border between the United States and Mexico. Early in his presidency, Trump issued executive orders aiming to limit immigration into America. Many officials and representatives have been working against his planned reform by passing sanctuary laws and refusing to cooperate with U.S. Immigration and Customs Enforcement operations.

Once Routine, Immigration Check-Ins Are Now High Stakes

BY LIZ ROBBINS | APRIL 11, 2017

FOR YEARS, it was an uneventful ritual. Unauthorized immigrants who weren't considered a priority for deportation would meet with an Immigration and Customs Enforcement officer and be told simply, "See you next year."

The deportation officers, as they are known, were employing prosecutorial discretion, which let them free up resources and detention center space to focus on the deportation of convicted criminals.

Now, under President Trump, the stakes of these meetings have changed. What was routine is now roulette.

Mr. Trump issued an executive order in January broadening the definition of deportable offenses to include all immigrants living in the country illegally. It has affected all levels of enforcement, including the check-in where people wait to go before an immigration judge or appear with pending appeals and petitions or final orders of removal.

Nobody wants to be the next Guadalupe García de Rayos, the Arizona woman who was deported to Mexico after her routine check-in with ICE officials in February. She had been checking in annually since she was caught using a fake Social Security number in 2008.

"Every immigration lawyer in the U.S. has this uncertainty with clients now," said Kerry Bretz, a veteran New York lawyer. Previously, he said, he told his clients: "Don't worry about it. You're going to walk in, you're going to walk out, you're going to renew your work authorization and get on with your life."

KEVIN HAGEN FOR THE NEW YORK TIMES

Ravi Ragbir, center, brought a show of force to his check-in with Immigration and Customs Enforcement in Lower Manhattan. The City Council members Jumaane D. Williams, left, and Ydanis Rodriguez walked arm in arm with him afterward.

Now, he said, it's his ethical duty to warn clients before a check-in to get their affairs in order. "Because you might not come out," he said.

Meredith Kalman, a lawyer for Mr. Bretz's firm, said that as she was leaving a check-in last month in Manhattan, an officer gave her this warning: "It's a whole new world, Counselor."

According to Ms. Kalman, the officer told her during the meeting, "I'm sorry, I'm getting pressure because my title is deportation officer — my job is to deport people."

Immigration agency officials insist that they still focus on the deportation of people who were convicted of crimes and pose a threat to their community. However, Rachael Yong Yow, a spokeswoman for the ICE New York field office, said, "All of those in violation of the immigration laws may be subject to immigration arrest, detention and, if found removable by final order, removal from the United States."

That is what should be happening, said Daniel Stein, the president of the Federation for American Immigration Reform, which supports stricter immigration controls. "If you are here and removable, you are living on borrowed time," he said.

Mr. Stein said prosecutorial discretion, generally used in criminal law, should not technically cover ICE check-ins since ICE was not giving people legal status to stay in the country at these meetings, only granting them an administrative delay.

Cheryl R. David, a New York immigration lawyer, sees the chances for such a delay dwindling. "There's definitely been a culture shift," she said.

"ICE is more inclined to enforce, from their perspective, the immigration law," Ms. David added, "and if you have a final order of removal, you're going to have to try and rectify it."

Or else, she said, deportation will follow.

There seems to be no consistent policy from one field office to the next, lawyers say. The immigration agency was not immediately able to provide statistics regarding those who were detained or deported as a result of their check-ins, or how the frequency of those check-ins had changed.

Last month, Mr. Bretz accompanied a client, a 49-year-old real estate business owner from the former Soviet Union, to his check-in in Manhattan, bringing a thick file of testimonials from his client's associates along with pictures of his children. Mr. Bretz said that his client had no criminal record, and that attempts to rectify what he claimed was an immigration officer's mistake in adjusting his status more than 20 years earlier had failed.

For the seventh straight year, the man was told that he could come back in a year.

Another lawyer in Mr. Bretz's firm, Tiffany Javier, had the opposite experience in Hartford. Her client, a 44-year-old man from Kenya, had arrived in 1993 on a visa but had overstayed. He became a nurse, he paid taxes, and he was raising a stepson with his second wife.

But years earlier, a judge had rejected his request for a green card after he married his first wife, suspecting that the marriage was fraudulent. He had been checking in quarterly, until February, when he was given a month to buy his own ticket back to Kenya. He left in mid-March.

The experience led Ms. Javier to believe that now, prosecutorial discretion was "out the window." She said some immigration officers "feel emboldened where they can pretty much do what they want."

The uncertain climate has led to a new trend: spirited protests by advocates, clergy and city officials surrounding a check-in.

In March in Newark, a 59-year-old man who had come in illegally from Mexico in 1991 arrived for a check-in with an entourage that included Senator Robert Menendez, a Democrat from New Jersey, and Cardinal Joseph W. Tobin of the Newark Archdiocese. Cardinal Tobin, an outspoken defender of immigrant's rights, gave a brief speech imploring the ICE officials who would decide the man's fate to "not only see his face, but see ours as well."

The man, Catalino Guerrero, had been checking in annually since 2011 because an asylum application someone had filed by mistake had been rejected. He had suffered a stroke, and because of his health was granted a stay of removal. This time, he was told to return in three months while his lawyers pursued another avenue for him to stay in the country.

KEVIN HAGEN FOR THE NEW YORK TIMES

Supporters of Mr. Ragbir at a rally in Manhattan on March 9, 2017. Mr. Ragbir came from Trinidad and Tobago in 1991 and was ordered deported after being convicted of wire fraud in 2000.

At another protest outside the Jacob K. Javits Federal Building in Lower Manhattan, more than 100 advocates from the New Sanctuary Movement of New York were rallying around their executive director, Ravi Ragbir, who was fighting his own deportation. Mr. Ragbir, 56, came from Trinidad and Tobago in 1991 and had been a lawful permanent resident when he was convicted of wire fraud in 2000. After he served his sentence, he was ordered deported and detained by immigration officials.

In 2011, the New York field office of ICE granted him a stay of removal, which he most recently renewed until 2018.

On March 9, an ICE officer ordered him to return in a month with proof that he had applied for travel documents with Trinidad and Tobago's consulate in New York. He did that, and on Thursday, the enforcement agency did exercise discretion — allowing Mr. Ragbir to check in in January 2018.

In the ninth-floor waiting room of the federal building in Manhattan, where ICE check-ins take place, the worry among people of all ages and nationalities was palpable last month. Two televisions were turned to CNN; Mr. Trump flashed on the screen. From one of the four unmarked doors — no one knew where to look — an ICE officer would emerge and call a name.

Ramesh Palaniandi, a legal permanent resident from Guyana who had served a brief sentence for burglary, went in that day, but did not re-emerge. He was taken to a detention center after his ICE check-in, leaving his crying wife, Janice Hoseine, behind. A month later he was released with his case still pending.

But in Latham, N.Y., at the federal immigration office in the Hudson Valley, one lawyer was heartened by the treatment of his client's case. Maria Martínez-Chacón, a native of El Salvador, has been under an order of supervision since February, when ICE picked up her husband, Ramiro, for having re-entered the country illegally.

She has two children who are United States citizens, and was told to return on April 19. According to her lawyer, Nicholas E. Tishler, Ms. Martínez-Chacón has a good case for asylum.

"The people I have come into contact with so far have exercised their discretion in a humane manner," Mr. Tishler said, "and I hope it continues."

JACEY FORTIN CONTRIBUTED REPORTING.

Without New Laws or Walls, Trump Presses the Brake on Legal Immigration

BY MIRIAM JORDAN | DEC. 20, 2017

A SCIENTIST recruited by the renowned Cleveland Clinic is stuck in India because his visa is delayed. An entrepreneur courted by Silicon Valley companies had his application denied. Many green card applicants have new interviews to pass.

The Trump administration has pursued its immigration agenda loudly and noticeably, ramping up arrests of undocumented immigrants, barring most travel from several majority-Muslim countries and pressing the case for a border wall.

But it has also quietly, and with much less resistance, slowed many forms of legal immigration without the need for Congress to rescind a single visa program enshrined in the law.

Immigration and State Department officials are more closely scrutinizing, and have started more frequently denying, visas for people seeking to visit the United States on business, as well as for those recruited by American companies, according to lawyers representing visa seekers. Foreigners already in the United States whose employers wish to extend their stays are also facing new hurdles.

"I call this the real wall," said Anastasia Tonello, the president-elect of the American Immigration Lawyers Association. "The wall is being built."

The changes show how the Trump administration has managed to carry out the least attention-grabbing, but perhaps farthest-reaching, portion of the president's immigration plans: cutting the number of people entering the United States each year as temporary workers or permanent residents.

The administration has put into practice the philosophy President Trump laid out in a pair of executive orders billed as protecting the nation from terrorism and its workers from foreign competition.

One of them, the "Buy American, Hire American" order, singles out the H-1B visa program for skilled workers who otherwise would not be allowed into the country. Hailed by proponents as vital to American innovation, H-1Bs have also been derided as a way to displace United States workers with cheaper foreign labor; in one highly publicized case, some Disney employees were told to train their foreign replacements if they wanted severance payments.

Each year, 85,000 H-1Bs, which are valid for three to six years, are available to companies, according to a ceiling set by Congress. Demand far outstrips supply when the economy is healthy, prompting the government to hold a lottery.

But now even applicants lucky enough to be chosen are drawing more scrutiny.

T.J. KIRKPATRICK FOR THE NEW YORK TIMES

The Cleveland Clinic, one of many employers affected by President Trump's tougher approach toward immigration, has faced challenges securing visas for foreign-born specialists.

Officials are asking for extra details about applicants' education and work history, the position to be filled and the employer, requiring the company to amass many additional documents, which can postpone a decision by several months.

For H-1Bs, the number of such "requests for evidence" from January to August this year jumped 44 percent compared with the same period last year, according to the most recent data from United States Citizenship and Immigration Services.

So far, the government is still greenlighting most H-1B applications that survive the lottery, but the approval rate is inching down.

For the first two months of this fiscal year, October and November, 86 percent and 82 percent of H-1B applications were approved. That compares with 93 percent and 92 percent for the same months last year. The data does not reflect companies that give up after receiving requests for more evidence.

EROS HOAGLAND FOR THE NEW YORK TIMES

H-1B visa petitions arriving at a government processing center in Laguna Niguel, Calif. As a candidate, President Trump vowed to end the visa program.

Once a company has spent thousands of dollars in legal fees to petition for a worker, "there is huge discouragement after an R.F.E. is issued," said Roxanne Levine, an immigration lawyer in New York, "because of the massive extra time, effort and money required to respond."

L. Francis Cissna, the immigration agency's new director, said in an interview that if there are more requests for evidence, "that is perfectly rational and perfectly appropriate."

"We are looking at the entire program to ensure the entire thing is administered well and in conformity with congressional intent," he said.

He recently met with a group of displaced American workers in Florida, including some laid off by Disney. The meeting was arranged by Sara Blackwell, an employment lawyer who leads a group called Protect U.S. Workers. "The administration has done much more for American workers, but I hope to see much more soon," Ms. Blackwell said.

Immigration lawyers and companies seeking the visas say that some of the decisions appear arbitrary.

After responding to requests for evidence, a consulting firm that applied for an H-1B for an energy expert from Britain received a denial stating that the skills for the position "do not appear to be of such complexity, uniqueness or specialization as to require the attainment of a bachelor's degree," a prerequisite for the visa.

Kristen Albertson, the operations manager at the firm, called the outcome "egregious."

"We apply only when it's a strong case and essential to our business," she said of the applicant, who is a graduate of the University of Chicago.

An H-1B visa for an Indian scientist recruited by the Cleveland Clinic for his expertise in cellular biology is stuck in "administrative processing" in New Delhi, meaning it is undergoing further review that could stretch into months. "His team's projects are now on hold due to the delay," said Janice Bianco, an official at the Cleveland Clinic who handles applications for foreigners.

She said a visa for a pediatric geneticist hired in the spring took three months to be issued — in the past, it would have taken about three weeks — forcing the hospital to reroute some patients to other facilities.

The State Department, which has handled the Cleveland Clinic visa requests, said in a statement that "consular officers have the discretion to request additional screening in any case."

Other types of visas are also tougher to get now. During trips to Silicon Valley, Vladimir Eremeev of Russia was encouraged to establish a branch of his cloud-based technology company, Ivideon, in the United States. In Europe, Ivideon employs 150 people, and Philips, the Dutch multinational, sells a camera powered by its technology.

Mr. Eremeev drew up plans, which his lawyer in New York detailed in a 347-page visa application. He was applying for an L-1A visa, awarded to executives transferring to the United States.

"Sounds and looks great, but it didn't help me obtain a visa," Mr. Eremeev said in a phone interview.

Among other things, the immigration agency stated that the office leased by Mr. Eremeev did not appear to be suited for a "business that would require the employment of a manager or executive." His lawyer provided details and pictures of the space.

Ultimately, the government denied the petition, stating that the "organizational structure" presented did not support the "managerial or executive position" that Mr. Eremeev was to fill.

"You are going in circles," said the lawyer, Oksana Bandrivska, "and it's getting harder to win cases."

Russell Harrison, director of government relations for IEEE-USA, a society of technology professionals, applauded the administration's efforts to tackle visa abuse. However, he said, a blanket approach could stifle American competitiveness.

"They seem to be against anyone coming in, which is a simplistic view," Mr. Harrison said. "There are some incredibly talented people not born in this country, and they are being treated just like other workers who are cheap."

Some lawyers said they had also seen more scrutiny of H-2B visas, the seasonal work permits that Mr. Trump uses to staff his Mar-a-Lago club in Florida. Jeff Joseph, a lawyer in Aurora, Colo., said the government was more often denying visas for companies that sought the visas season after season. (Mar-a-Lago uses them only during winters.)

The government's argument, Mr. Joseph said, is that those companies are trying to import temporary workers to fill permanent jobs that should go to Americans. But he said his clients faced a shortage of local labor year after year to fill jobs in construction, lodging, landscaping and amusement parks.

Other changes affect foreigners already working or living in the United States on H-1Bs or other temporary permits.

Those sponsored by their employers for a green card, or legal permanent residency, must pass in-person interviews, a reversal of a 20-year-old policy that is likely to exacerbate a long backlog in green card applications. A memo from the immigration agency said the change was in line with the executive order to safeguard the nation from terrorism.

The administration said this month that it planned to eliminate a program established during the Obama administration that allows international entrepreneurs to stay in the United States for up to five years. The administration also said it would eliminate a two-year-old program that granted work permits for spouses of H-1B workers. And it recently announced plans to restrict the ability of foreign students to work temporarily in the United States after they graduate.

Another change affects green card holders who enlist in the military. Since the Sept. 11, 2001, terrorist attacks, military service has provided a faster path to citizenship than applying as a civilian, typically taking just 10 weeks.

In October, the Pentagon enacted new procedures that substantially slow the process by adding several layers of vetting. The change affects thousands of immigrants who have already enlisted because they cannot start training before clearing the background checks.

The Pentagon said the new measures were needed to ensure that terrorists do not infiltrate the military. But Margaret Stock, an immigration lawyer and retired lieutenant colonel in the Army, said the military would suffer. "They are turning away green card holders with language, cybersecurity and other skills that the United States military needs," she said.

What Can the U.S. Learn From How Other Countries Handle Immigration?

BY QUOCTRUNG BUI AND CAITLIN DICKERSON | FEB. 16, 2018

EVERY COUNTRY regulates immigration in its own imperfect way. Some countries have populations that are 80 percent foreign-born but offer no pathway to permanency. Other countries put up huge barriers to citizenship except for people whose parents were born there.

In the United States, the Senate has struggled, unsuccessfully so far, to pass an immigration reform bill. But the debate has put nearly every category of immigration on the table, from smaller, targeted programs such as Deferred Action for Childhood Arrivals, Temporary Protected Status and the Diversity Immigrant Visa, to big pillars of the immigration system like work-related and family-based migration.

President Trump has called for a shift from what currently makes the American immigration system distinct: its focus on family ties, a framework that accounts for two-thirds of all residency visas, more than any other country. Instead, he and many Republicans would like most visas to be distributed based on employability, with a preference for those who are highly skilled, like doctors, engineers or entrepreneurs.

"In many ways the U.S. immigration system is a relic of the past," said Justin Gest, a professor at George Mason University who studies comparative immigration policy, referring to how public opinion has changed since 1965, when the family-based system was established. "It is far more generous than I think the spirit of the United States is today."

Simply put, the purpose of an immigration policy is to decide what types of people to allow inside the border. What would it look like if the United States adopted rules more like those of Canada, Japan or Qatar? Compare the policies below.

THE MIX IF WE LOOKED MORE LIKE CANADA

In 2011, Canada and Australia relied heavily on immigrants who were admitted based on employability, many of whom were allowed to stay permanently. Both countries used a merit-based point system to determine who qualified, assigning a number of points to criteria such as education, language skills and employment history.

Mr. Trump has said that he would like to emulate the Canadian and Australian systems. But Mr. Gest pointed to a blind spot the size of Ohio — the seventh-most populous state — that could be obscuring how similar the systems already are: undocumented immigrants, who are highly represented in the United States in many low-skill industries like farming and construction.

"If you think of the undocumented as 11 to 12 million temporary low-skilled laborers, then you have a system that looks a little bit more like Canada" in terms of temporary workers, he said. (In fact, Canada and Australia have a much greater proportion of temporary workers than the United States.)

But a merit-based system doesn't necessarily result in economic payoff, because skills don't always lead to a job. For example, Canada has struggled to keep its merit-based workers employed since 1967, when the policy was first established.

That's because some of the very skills and credentials that ushered immigrants into the country were unrecognized once they arrived, so many ended up unemployed or underemployed.

Another reason President Trump might not want to rely too heavily on Canada or Australia as models: Both countries allow in far more immigrants as a percentage of their population. If the United States were to follow their lead, it would involve admitting millions more people.

OR MORE LIKE EUROPE

Historically, most immigrants in Europe have been other Europeans.

The European Union allows people to relocate between countries with a level of freedom that is unmatched elsewhere in the world, greatly widening employment pools.

Middle Eastern conflict has created an exception in recent years, spurring a big influx of asylum seekers from war-torn countries. But humanitarian migrants typically make up only a small proportion of Europe's foreign-born population.

Mercosur, a trade bloc in South America, functions like the E.U., though it allows people to live outside their home countries for only two years at a time, after which they must apply for permission to stay permanently.

It might help to imagine that these partnerships are like Nafta — the policy between the United States, Mexico and Canada that lowers barriers for trade, which President Trump has threatened to eliminate — but instead of goods, the agreements apply to people.

In a system like that, Americans looking for work would be able to expand their searches into Canada and Mexico, but they would also compete against Canadian and Mexican candidates for jobs in the United States.

OR LIKE JAPAN AND SOUTH KOREA

South Korea and Japan are so stringent with immigration that they make the United States look lenient. This is partly because of a desire to preserve their cultures, a goal echoed by some conservative groups in the United States.

For example, the Japanese government once offered thousands of dollars to immigrants of Japanese descent to leave the country. And very few people become South Korean citizens without family ties; doing so requires years of residence, an in-person language proficiency test and a written test on customs, history and culture.

On top of stoking racial tensions, these policies have created demographic problems for South Korea and Japan. Both countries' populations are aging rapidly, social services are underfunded, and many industries face labor shortages.

Some unusual policies, such as Japan's practice of granting citizenship based on a parent's Japanese nationality instead of where babies are born, have created situations where three generations of a family may not be Japanese citizens despite having lived in the country all their lives.

OR LIKE THE GULF STATES

The Gulf states allow a huge immigrant influx to meet the demand for cheap, low-skilled labor, but almost all of the immigrants are temporary, and they have few rights or protections.

In Qatar, for example, roughly 80 percent of the population is foreign-born. Without them, the skyscrapers of Doha or the 2022 World Cup, for which the government has promised to build more than half a dozen new stadiums, would not be possible. And the Qatari government has been accused of human rights abuses against those workers.

The only way that governments can sustain these heavy immigrant populations is by withholding the generous resources that are granted to ordinary citizens, such as free health care, free college tuition and marriage allowances.

Most Americans would not be comfortable with this approach, said Morris Levy, a political scientist at the University of Southern California who studies public opinion on immigration. "People dislike the idea of a permanent second-class citizen," he said. "It goes back to a core set of values that people think of as really elemental to being American."

THE FUTURE IS PROBABLY SOMEWHERE IN THE MIDDLE

Based on the current debate, any solution that Congress agrees on will probably fall somewhere between international models. It could follow some trends that are occurring worldwide.

For example, in many countries, including Canada and Australia, there has been a shift away from exclusively merit-based systems to ones that also consider whether someone has a job offer — something currently done in the United States.

For purposes of immigration, the United States could narrow its definition of family, which is wider than that of any other country, to exclude siblings or adult children who are married.

Although current American policies around family-based migration are the most generous in the world, the results look much different in practice because of limits on the number of visas that can be granted in each category.

"There is a certain mindlessness to family immigration when you take into account eligibility and time," said Demetrios G. Papademetriou, co-founder of the Migration Policy Institute, a research organization. "Someone qualifies, but it may take 20 years before a visa is open to them."

"There is a major undisputed advantage to family immigration, chain migration; it's become apparently a dirty word," he said. "You have someone here who will show you the ropes, who will take you in that can set up employment for you. When it comes to immigrant integration, family is very important."

You could envision a merit-based system that incorporates characteristics of our current system. It could grant points to people who have family members in the United States, or who come from countries that are not highly represented in the current population.

In that case, it might be desirable to pay attention to the weight each category is given and to adjust based on economic and social outcomes.

"That is how you keep a point selection system," Mr. Papademetriou said. "Everything else is just blind faith or politics. Our system that exists today is just politics."

While the sputtering negotiations are frustrating for many people, especially for those caught up in the system, academics agree that, in general, these decisions should not be rushed.

"Immigration is social engineering," said Mr. Gest, the George Mason University professor. "You're building the population of the future."

Is America a 'Nation of Immigrants'? Immigration Agency Says No

BY MIRIAM JORDAN | FEB. 22, 2018

LOS ANGELES — The federal agency that issues green cards and grants citizenship to people from foreign countries has stopped characterizing the United States as "a nation of immigrants."

The director of United States Citizenship and Immigration Services informed employees in a letter on Thursday that its mission statement had been revised to "guide us in the years ahead." Gone was the phrase that described the agency as securing "America's promise as a nation of immigrants."

The original mission statement, created in 2005, said, "U.S.C.I.S. secures America's promise as a nation of immigrants by providing accurate and useful information to our customers, granting immigration and citizenship benefits, promoting an awareness and understanding of citizenship, and ensuring the integrity of our immigration system."

The new version says: "U.S. Citizenship and Immigration Services administers the nation's lawful immigration system, safeguarding its integrity and promise by efficiently and fairly adjudicating requests for immigration benefits while protecting Americans, securing the homeland and honoring our values."

The agency director, L. Francis Cissna, who was appointed by the Trump administration, described the revision as a "simple, straightforward statement" that "clearly defines the agency's role in our country's lawful immigration system and the commitment we have to the American people."

Mr. Cissna did not mention in his letter that he had removed the phrase "nation of immigrants," which was popularized by a book by President John F. Kennedy and is frequently used to convey America's multiculturalism.

However, Mr. Cissna did note that he had eliminated the word "customers" in describing the foreign nationals whom the agency serves, "a reminder that we are always working for the American people."

León Rodríguez, director of the agency from 2014 to 2017, said the revision of the mission statement marked "a particularly sad turn of history."

"We should not forget that under the discarded mission statement, the integrity and national security functions of U.S.C.I.S. grew — dramatically so — showing that we could be both a welcoming nation and a safe one," Mr. Rodríguez said. "We should stop to reflect about the many opportunities that America will lose because of the attitudes reflected in this statement, and ask ourselves whether this is really the country we want to be."

Ira Mehlman, a spokesman for the Federation for American Immigration Reform, which favors restricting immigration, applauded the change.

"A nation of immigrants isn't a mission statement," he said, "it's a slogan."

"The biggest problem with our immigration system is that it lacks a clear national interest objective," he added.

As director of U.S.C.I.S., Mr. Cissna has promoted an agenda that reflects the Trump administration's skeptical and often hard-line stance on immigration. The agency has increased scrutiny of visa applications for foreign workers whom American companies seek to hire; it has changed the asylum application process to discourage people from seeking safe haven in the United States; and it has added steps to the process for foreigners already in the country to obtain legal permanent residency, or a green card.

U.S.C.I.S., a unit of the Department of Homeland Security, reviews petitions of foreign nationals who seek to visit, work, reside and find refuge in the United States. It also processes citizenship applications, which have surged since President Trump won the election in 2016.

In his letter to his staff, Mr. Cissna wrote, "We are also responsible for ensuring that those who naturalize are dedicated to this country, share our values, assimilate into our communities, and understand their responsibility to help preserve our freedom and liberty."

Published posthumously, Kennedy's "A Nation of Immigrants" highlighted the contribution of immigrants when the country was engulfed in a debate over the direction of its immigration policy.

The phrase appears at least as far back as 1874, in an editorial published in The Daily State Journal of Alexandria, which praised a bill passed by the Virginia Senate appropriating $15,000 to encourage European immigration. "We are a nation of immigrants and immigrants' children," it said.

Immigrant advocates today invoke the phrase to remind the country that most Americans have an ancestor who was once a newcomer to the United States.

Did Melania Trump Merit an 'Einstein Visa'? Probably, Immigration Lawyers Say

BY MIRIAM JORDAN | MARCH 4, 2018

IT IS KNOWN AS the "Einstein visa." Nuclear scientists, Nobel laureates and doctors get it. But so do acrobats, stunt men, event planners — and plenty of models.

Each year, thousands of foreigners try to persuade government officials that they are among the best in their field. The prize if they succeed: a green card, and with it, the right to live permanently in the United States.

Reports that the first lady, Melania Trump, received an immigrant visa reserved for "individuals with extraordinary ability" in 2001, when she was a model, have thrust the EB-1 visa program into the spotlight. The news, first reported by The Washington Post, raised questions about whether Mrs. Trump had truly qualified for the visa.

But several immigration lawyers rebuffed those questions, saying the requirements for the EB-1 immigrant visa leave far more room for interpretation than its nickname and its best-and-brightest reputation suggest.

While the program may be the pinnacle of the merit-based immigration policies supported by critics of the visa lottery and family-based migration — indeed, by President Trump himself — the decision of what constitutes merit, while based on established criteria, is ultimately subjective and often surprising.

"Recipients are supposed to be the best of the best," said Rita Sostrin, a Los Angeles-based lawyer who has written extensively about EB-1s, "but meeting the criteria is no guarantee. An adjudication officer makes a judgment call."

The "extraordinary ability" immigrant visa category is one of the few visas for which an applicant does not require an employer or family sponsor. Only 5,530 people received a green card through that program in the fiscal year that ended in September 2016, the latest for which data is available, out of some one million issued. In 2001, when Mrs. Trump got hers, even fewer were granted.

Marshall Cohen, a lawyer in Atlanta who specializes in EB-1s for world-ranked track and field athletes, said that he would not have hesitated to represent Mrs. Trump.

"I am assuming she made a lot of money, got a lot of press and was on the cover of magazines," he said. "She was probably a pretty easy case." Mrs. Trump, then Melania Knauss, appeared on the cover of British GQ in 2000, the year she petitioned for the EB-1, and was featured in Sports Illustrated and other magazines later that year.

"Do we need more foreign fashion models? Some might say no," said Mr. Cohen, who led a panel titled "Proving Extraordinary Ability Is Extraordinarily Challenging" at a recent immigration lawyers' conference. "We might need more chemical engineers. But if there is a fashion model at the top of her field, she could qualify."

Petitioners for the EB-1, which was created as part of the Immigration Act of 1990, face a two-part test. The United States Citizenship and Immigration Services first must determine whether a candidate has presented evidence to satisfy three out of 10 criteria, such as publishing material in professional publications or other major media, appearing in artistic exhibitions or commanding a high salary.

Once those are met, the decision comes down to a vague and undefined "final merits determination" by the immigration agency.

"That is the mystery; nobody knows what it is," said Ms. Sostrin, the lawyer in Los Angeles, who recently secured EB-1s for an award-winning stunt performer and a high-end events planner.

What is clear is that extraordinary intelligence is not necessary — nor sufficient on its own — to get one. Indeed, even Albert Einstein might have not qualified for an EB-1 before winning the Nobel Prize.

TOM BRENNER/THE NEW YORK TIMES

Melania Trump at the White House last month. Reports that Mrs. Trump received a visa reserved for "individuals with extraordinary ability" in 2001, when she was a model, raised questions about whether she truly qualified.

A few years ago, Ms. Sostrin distributed a résumé to immigration lawyers at a conference without revealing that it was Einstein's, or at least one devised from his career accomplishments. Ms. Sostrin asked them to assess the likelihood that he would be approved for an extraordinary ability visa.

The consensus was that it would be very challenging: The résumé, for a tutor and patent examiner turned professor, listed only a handful of the most important scientific works Einstein had published by 1920, more than a decade into his academic career.

"The notion that you somehow have to be a genius or Einstein is utter fiction," said Chris Wright, a lawyer based in Los Angeles. "We have succeeded with models no more accomplished than Melania Trump."

While the majority of applicants and recipients have titles like "space scientist," "cancer researcher" and "software engineer," many have less scholarly pursuits. In 2012, Mr. Wright represented Shera

Béchard, a Canadian model and Playboy Playmate who successfully petitioned for an EB-1. In her petition, Mr. Wright included scantily clad photographs of Ms. Béchard.

"When it's a glamorous model and pictures show cleavage rather than research, people assume there is something underhanded going on," said Mr. Wright, who said that he had also obtained the visas for a racecar driver, a hair dresser and a tennis player.

For Glenn Boswell, a stunt performer and director used to jumping out of buildings and moving vehicles, getting the EB-1 was a relative cake walk.

His lawyer filed a 439-page petition in 2016 detailing Mr. Boswell's achievements, which include credits in "Unbroken," "The Matrix" and "The Hobbit," and he received approval within a week. "I was really excited when it came," Mr. Boswell, 60, said in a phone interview from his native Australia. He had no idea he had joined an exclusive club.

Daniel Riffner, 35, an acrobat for Cirque du Soleil in Las Vegas, compiled a dossier in 2009 about his 25-year career, packed with medals, pictures of his high-wire acts and recommendations from coaches. Kinan Azmeh, 41, a Syrian clarinetist in Brooklyn who is a member of Yo-Yo Ma's Silk Road Ensemble, applied in 2012. Both received green cards.

Mr. Trump has championed an immigration overhaul that would replace the current family-based system, which he derides as "chain migration," with one based on merit, emphasizing skill and educational level. His proposal would have made it impossible for the first lady to sponsor her parents for a green card, which she did after obtaining permanent legal residency and becoming a citizen herself. Meanwhile, highly skilled people, whether scientists or entrepreneurs, often get turned down when they apply to work and live in the country.

Especially under the Trump administration, immigration lawyers said, U.S.C.I.S. has made a habit of making requests for further evidence before deciding the fate of an applicant. The lawyers also said that scholars and scientists have a tougher time winning approval than models, actors and athletes.

Elissa Taub, a lawyer in Memphis who secured the EB-1 for the German gymnast, said that some of her denials "burn me to this day," like that of a nuclear astrophysicist who had produced groundbreaking work at a national lab. Immigration officials said his title on the job was not senior enough to merit the EB-1.

"We lost a great scientific mind due to this crazy decision," she said of the scholar, who returned to India.

In another case, U.S.C.I.S. acknowledged that a Chinese researcher had fulfilled three criteria to qualify, but that "scientists who have risen to the very top of the field have garnered citations numbered in the thousands," not in the hundreds, as he had shown. He was denied.

Despite ample documentation and detailed letters from world-renowned experts supporting the petition of a molecular oncologist who studies drug-resistant cancer, U.S.C.I.S. questioned whether her scholarship was significant. After her lawyer submitted further evidence, she was approved.

"These are people we should be rolling out the red carpet for," said David Soloway, the lawyer who handled the case.

"Most people would readily say that it makes sense for someone who is extraordinarily skilled in the sciences to be admitted to this country," Mr. Soloway added. "But in modeling? Really?"

Immigration Agency Rails Against Oakland Mayor's Warning of Raids

BY THOMAS FULLER | FEB. 28, 2018

SAN FRANCISCO — A top federal official likened Mayor Libby Schaaf of Oakland to a "gang lookout" on Wednesday, saying her warning of an impending, large-scale arrest operation had given immigrants in the United States illegally the opportunity to flee.

Ms. Schaaf had announced on Saturday that she had learned through "unofficial channels" that the federal Immigrations and Customs Enforcement agency, or ICE, was planning arrests in the area.

"I know that Oakland is a city of law-abiding immigrants and families who deserve to live free from the constant threat of arrest and deportation," she said in a statement that circulated widely on social media over the weekend. "I believe it is my duty and moral obligation as mayor to give those families fair warning when that threat appears imminent."

The mayor's warnings proved correct. Since Sunday night, ICE officers have arrested more than 150 people in Northern California in an operation ICE said was targeting "public safety threats."

But ICE officials said the mayor's warning jeopardized officers' safety, and said that hundreds more undocumented immigrants they had planned to arrest may have eluded the agents after the tip-off.

In a statement, the agency's acting director, Thomas D. Homan, called Ms. Schaaf's announcement a "reckless decision" made for political purposes.

Speaking on Wednesday morning on Fox News, Mr. Homan said Ms. Schaaf's warning was "no better than a gang lookout yelling 'Police!' when a police cruiser comes in the neighborhood, except she did it to an entire community."

The fight between ICE officials and Ms. Schaaf added a fresh layer of acrimony to a battle between the Trump administration, which has stepped up efforts to detain and deport unauthorized immigrants, and California officials determined to resist the president's agenda.

State laws passed in the last year limit the ability of local police to cooperate with federal immigration officials, and require employers to warn their workers whenever ICE makes a request for employee paperwork, which could give any undocumented employee the chance to leave before federal agents detect their presence.

President Trump, meanwhile, has singled out California for attacks and derision, saying its policies were letting dangerous immigrants live freely in the United States. Mr. Homan, the ICE chief, had promised to increase enforcement in California, saying in January that the state had "better hold on tight."

James Schwab, a spokesman for ICE in San Francisco, said agents were targeting around 1,000 people in the area, which appeared to be one of the largest operations since Mr. Trump took office. Mr. Homan blamed the mayor's warning for agents not being able to detain 800 people they had targeted in recent days.

One official briefed on the plans for the operation at the Department of Homeland Security, which includes ICE, said that ICE agents typically find only about 30 percent of their targets during any large sweep. The official, who was not authorized to discuss the operation, declined to be identified.

The 30 percent rate would suggest that while some immigrants may have benefited from the tip-off, it is unlikely that 800 of them did, as Mr. Homan suggested.

Immigration advocates have occasionally sought to warn of rumors of impending ICE arrests, but Ms. Schaaf's decision was striking because it came from the mayor of one of California's largest cities.

Ms. Schaaf, the mayor since January 2015, has been a strong promoter of Oakland's diversity, including its large population of immigrants, who make up around a third of the city's 420,000 residents.

In an interview on Wednesday, the mayor said she did not regret her decision to issue advance warning.

JIM WILSON/THE NEW YORK TIMES

Protesters outside an ICE office. The agency said a warning from the Oakland mayor prevented its officers from arresting hundreds of undocumented immigrants.

"I still contend that what I did was both legal and moral," she said, batting away a suggestion made during Mr. Homan's appearance on Fox News that she could have obstructed justice. "I did not provide any specific detail that could have endangered law enforcement."

A Bay Area liberal standard-bearer in a decidedly liberal city, Ms. Schaaf has been an unshrinking critic of Mr. Trump, whom she has called the "bully in chief."

She said she interpreted the raids as both racist and politically motivated, targeting liberal California.

"The Trump administration and ICE officials have been very transparent that they are retaliating against California for its political position," she said.

The president, she said, "is trying to equate immigrants with dangerous criminals."

Although Ms. Schaaf said she had information that ICE had been targeting people in Oakland, she had not heard of any arrests taking place in the city.

Immigrant advocates reported arrests by ICE in Merced, Contra Costa, Sacramento, Monterey and Napa Counties — an area much broader than just the San Francisco Bay Area. On Wednesday, several dozen protesters gathered outside the ICE office in San Francisco, chanting support for undocumented immigrants and writing "KEEP FAMILIES TOGETHER" across an intersection.

While the Obama administration focused arrest efforts on undocumented immigrants who had committed crimes in the United States, Mr. Trump has made clear that anyone in the country without permission can be arrested. Last year, immigration arrests nationwide rose by more than a third from the previous year, in large part because officers have more freedom to detain unauthorized immigrants with no criminal record.

Still, the administration has made a point of highlighting the criminal pasts of undocumented immigrants. Around half of those arrested in Northern California in recent days had previous criminal convictions in addition to immigration violations, said Mr. Schwab, the ICE spokesman.

An ICE statement said some had lengthy criminal records, including one, Armando Nuñez-Salgado, whom the agency called a "documented Sureño gang member" who had been deported four times and who over the past 18 years had accumulated convictions — it listed burglary and hit-and-run causing injury — resulting in more than 15 years in prison.

Mr. Schwab would not say on Wednesday whether the arrest operation was continuing, but he said the agency would issue a statement once it was completed.

CAITLIN DICKERSON CONTRIBUTED REPORTING FROM NEW YORK.

Trump Administration Sues California Over Immigration Laws

BY KATIE BENNER AND JENNIFER MEDINA | MARCH 6, 2018

WASHINGTON — The Trump administration escalated what had been a war of words over California's immigration agenda, filing a lawsuit late Tuesday that amounted to a pre-emptive strike against the liberal state's so-called sanctuary laws.

The Justice Department sued California; Gov. Jerry Brown; and the state's attorney general, Xavier Becerra, over three state laws passed in recent months, saying they made it impossible for federal immigration officials to do their jobs and deport criminals who were born outside the United States. The Justice Department called the laws unconstitutional and asked a judge to block them.

The lawsuit was the department's boldest attack yet against California, one of the strongest opponents of the Trump administration's

JIM WILSON/THE NEW YORK TIMES

Gov. Jerry Brown was named in a lawsuit that seeks to block three California laws that may hinder the federal immigration agenda.

efforts to curb immigration. It also served as a warning to Democratic lawmakers and elected officials nationwide who have enacted sanctuary policies that provide protections for undocumented immigrants.

"The Department of Justice and the Trump administration are going to fight these unjust, unfair and unconstitutional policies that have been imposed on you," Attorney General Jeff Sessions planned to say on Wednesday at a law enforcement event in Sacramento, according to prepared remarks. "I believe that we are going to win."

The battle pits President Trump and Mr. Sessions, immigration hard-liners, against Mr. Brown and Mr. Becerra, who have emerged as outspoken adversaries who have helped energize opposition to Mr. Trump and vowed to preserve the progressive values that they believe California embodies.

The lawsuit claims that the statutes "reflect a deliberate effort by California to obstruct the United States' enforcement of federal immigration law." It also says the laws regulate private entities that want to cooperate with the federal authorities and "impede consultation and communication between federal and state law enforcement officials."

Mr. Brown called the lawsuit a "political stunt."

"At a time of unprecedented political turmoil, Jeff Sessions has come to California to further divide and polarize America," Mr. Brown said in a statement. "Jeff, these political stunts may be the norm in Washington, but they don't work here. SAD!!!"

California began battling the Trump administration even before Mr. Trump took office, standing in opposition on a number of issues, including marijuana, environmental regulations and taxes. But immigration has proved to be the most contentious fight, with local officials assuring undocumented immigrants that they would do all they could to protect them.

Last year, California enacted the sanctuary laws, which restrict when and how local law enforcement can cooperate with federal immigration enforcement officers.

Both Mr. Sessions and Mr. Trump have threatened to pull federal grant money from cities and states that have sanctuary laws to protect undocumented immigrants. They argue that the policies flout federal laws and help criminals evade deportation.

And the Justice Department asked 23 jurisdictions across the country this year to provide documentation that they had not kept information from federal immigration authorities, or receive a subpoena for the information. It is also exploring possible criminal charges for local politicians who enact sanctuary policies.

The lawsuit filed on Tuesday evening in Federal District Court in Sacramento is the first against a local or state government over its immigration policies filed by the Justice Department under Mr. Sessions. Department officials said that they would not rule out the possibility of other lawsuits against local governments whose policies interfere with the federal government's authority on immigration. Colorado, Illinois, New Mexico, Oregon and Vermont have state sanctuary laws, as do cities and counties in more than a dozen states, according to the Center for Immigration Studies.

One, the California Values Act, strictly limits state and local agencies from sharing information with federal officers about criminals or suspects unless they have been convicted of serious crimes. The law, which took effect Jan. 1, was the centerpiece of the State Legislature's effort to thwart the Trump administration's immigration policies.

Soon after the law was enacted, Thomas D. Homan, the acting director of United States Immigration and Customs Enforcement, said that the state should expect to see "a lot more deportation officers" and that elected officials who support the policy should be arrested.

"We've got to start charging some of these politicians with crimes," he said. "These politicians can't make these decisions and be held unaccountable for people dying. I mean, we need to hold these politicians accountable for their actions."

Mr. Homan and three other immigration and border protection officials filed declarations with the suit claiming that California's laws had already negatively affected their work.

"The administration is just angry that a state has stood up to them — one that embraces diversity and inclusivity and is the sixth-largest economy in the world thanks to the hard-working immigrants who want to become American citizens," said Kevin de León, the leader of the California State Senate who wrote one of the sanctuary city laws named in the suit.

State lawmakers also passed the Immigrant Worker Protection Act, which prohibits local business from allowing immigration to gain access to employee records without a court order or subpoena. Mr. Becerra warned that anyone who violated the new law would face a fine of up to $10,000.

In the state budget bill, California lawmakers prohibited new contracts for immigration detention in the state and gave the state attorney general the power to monitor all state immigration detention centers.

The state and several local governments including the cities of San Francisco and Sacramento have also set up legal defense funds to help defend immigrants during deportation proceedings.

"I'm worried about the 'Dreamers,' hard-working immigrant families and law-abiding people who are just trying to make their way like the rest of us," Mayor Darrell Steinberg of Sacramento said this year when asked about the state's sanctuary legislation. "Civil disobedience is a respectful way to show your love for country."

Tensions between local and federal officials reached yet another height last week, when Mayor Libby Schaaf of Oakland publicly warned of coming large-scale immigration arrest operations. Mr. Homan compared the mayor to a "gang lookout yelling, "Police!" and said she gave people living in the United States illegally a chance to flee. He said her warning meant that the federal immigration authorities arrested about 200 people rather than the 1,000 they had anticipated rounding up.

Although Mr. Homan and other federal officials have warned about targeting California as it steps up immigration enforcement efforts, the number of people arrested has not drastically increased so far.

In December, the most recent month for which data is available, 1,715 unauthorized immigrants in California were arrested by ICE, compared with 1,379 in December 2016.

This is not the first time that the Justice Department has sued a state. During the Obama administration, the department filed a civil rights lawsuit against Georgia for segregating students with disabilities from classrooms and sued North Carolina over a bill to restrict bathroom use for transgender citizens. Mr. Sessions withdrew that lawsuit.

In a call with reporters on Tuesday night, Mr. Becerra said that he was confident California would prevail in court and that state and federal laws were not in conflict.

"In California, our state laws work in concert with federal law," he said. "Our teams work together to go after drug dealers and go after gang violence. What we won't do is change from being focused on public safety. We're in the business of public safety, not deportation."

Mr. Becerra said that he was not surprised by the news of the lawsuit and that the state had already won legal battles against the Trump administration. "We've seen this B-rated movie before," he said. "We're not doing their bidding on immigration enforcement and deportation."

KATIE BENNER REPORTED FROM WASHINGTON, AND JENNIFER MEDINA FROM LOS ANGELES.

ICE Spokesman Resigns, Saying He Could No Longer Spread Falsehoods for Trump Administration

BY JONAH ENGEL BROMWICH | MARCH 13, 2018

A SPOKESMAN FOR United States Immigration and Customs Enforcement has resigned, saying that he could no longer "bear the burden" of spreading falsehoods on behalf of the Trump administration.

The spokesman, James Schwab, who had worked for the agency's San Francisco Division, told news outlets Monday that his decision was prompted by false statements made by the agency on Feb. 27 and repeated by Attorney General Jeff Sessions last week.

The statements criticized the mayor of Oakland, Libby Schaaf, for her decision last month to warn city residents that a raid by federal immigration agents targeting roughly 1,000 people was imminent. The agency's deputy director, Thomas D. Homan, said that Ms. Schaaf's warning had helped "864 criminal aliens and public safety threats" to evade capture in the raid.

Mr. Sessions, in a visit to California last week, condemned Ms. Schaaf, a Democrat, and echoed the agency, asserting that her actions had allowed hundreds to escape.

Mr. Schwab said in interviews, first with The San Francisco Chronicle and then with CNN, that he had been frustrated by the remarks, and had quit "because I didn't want to perpetuate misleading facts."

"I asked them to change the information," he told The Chronicle, referring to the 864 people to whom the statement alluded. "I told them that the information was wrong, they asked me to deflect, and I didn't agree with that. Then I took some time and I quit."

He explained that the enforcement agency would have been unlikely to capture all of the roughly 1,000 undocumented immigrants in the area that it had targeted, and that it was incorrect to identify those who were not detained as threats to public safety.

"We were never going to pick up that many people," he said. "To say that 100 percent are dangerous criminals on the street, or that those people weren't picked up because of the misguided actions of the mayor, is just wrong."

Mr. Schwab did not immediately respond to requests for comment on Tuesday. He resigned last week, according to CNN.

"I just couldn't bear the burden — continuing on as a representative of the agency and charged with upholding integrity, knowing that information was false," he told CNN, adding that in his 16 years of experience in government he had never been asked to deflect when he knew something was inaccurate.

In a statement, Ms. Schaaf, whom President Trump criticized last week for alerting residents to the raid, praised Mr. Schwab "for speaking the truth while under intense pressure to lie."

"Our democracy depends on public servants who act with integrity and hold transparency in the highest regard," she added.

An official at the Department of Homeland Security, which includes ICE, briefed on the plans for the raid said last month that agents find only about 30 percent of their targets on average during large sweeps.

Mr. Schwab told CNN that he thought Ms. Schaaf's actions were "misguided," but that blaming her "for 800 dangerous people out there is just false."

ICE responded to Mr. Schwab's comments in a statement, saying, "Even one criminal alien on the street can put public safety at risk."

"As Director Homan stated, while we can't put a number on how many targets avoided arrest due to the mayor's warning, it clearly had an impact," the statement said. "While we disagree with Mr. Schwab on this issue, we appreciate his service and wish him well."

"If anyone wants to have a public argument over precisely how many dangerous criminal aliens eluded arrest because of the mayor's irresponsible actions, we are happy to have that debate," Sarah

Isgur Flores, a spokeswoman for the Justice Department, said in a statement.

In a 2016 interview, Mr. Schwab told The Marion Press, his hometown paper in Michigan, that he joined the Army after high school and was deployed to Korea for four years. His service lasted until 2005, according to his LinkedIn page, and he later joined the Department of Defense, where he became a public affairs specialist in 2011. He also worked at NASA for several years before joining ICE.

KATIE BENNER CONTRIBUTED REPORTING.

Glossary

alien A person living in a country where they are not a citizen.

asylum When someone is given protection by the government of a foreign country.

border patrol A law enforcement agency with the mission of preventing people from entering the United States illegally.

citizen A person who is entitled to the legal rights granted by a country, either through birth or naturalization.

Deferred Action for Childhood Arrivals An immigration policy allowing people who were brought into the USA illegally as children to remain in the country.

deportation The forced removal of a person from a country where they are not legally permitted to remain.

detention When someone is held in government custody.

Dreamers People who qualify to live in the United States under the Deferred Action for Childhood Arrivals policy.

emigration Leaving one country to live in another.

executive order A rule issued by the U.S. president which has the power of law.

green card A document giving permanent residence to an immigrant to the United States.

immigrant Someone who moves permanently to a new country.

Immigration and Customs Enforcement (ICE) A law enforcement agency with the mission of enforcing laws regarding border control, customs and immigration.

indictment A formal statement by a prosecuting authority, charging someone with an offense.

indigenous The original inhabitants of a country or area.

legislation A collection of laws relating to a certain subject.

persecution The harassment of people with different origins, religions or lifestyles.

prosecutorial discretion The authority of an agency to decide which cases to pursue and how to address them.

racial profiling The practice of law enforcement targeting people based on their race or ethnicity.

refugees People who are forced to leave their home country to escape war, persecution, natural disaster or other violence.

resident A person who is legally permitted to live in a country on a long-term basis.

sanctuary cities Cities that limit their cooperation with federal immigration law.

smuggling Bringing people or goods into a country illegally.

sponsor Someone who assumes responsibility for another person.

stay of removal A temporary postponement of deportation.

Supplemental Security Income A program that pays benefits to disabled and elderly people with limited income and resources.

temporary entry When someone is allowed to enter a country without the intention of establishing permanent residence.

undocumented immigrant Someone who enters or remains in a country illegally.

visa An endorsement in a passport allowing its holder to enter or remain in a country for a specified period of time.

Media Literacy Terms

"Media literacy" refers to the ability to access, understand, critically assess and create media. The following terms are important components of media literacy, and they will help you critically engage with the articles in this title.

angle The aspect of a news story that a journalist focuses on and develops.

balance A principle of journalism that both perspectives of an argument should be presented in a fair way.

bias A disposition of prejudice in favor of a certain idea, person or perspective.

column A type of story that is a regular feature, often on a recurring topic, written by the same journalist, generally known as a columnist.

commentary A type of story that is an expression of opinion on recent events by a journalist generally known as a commentator.

credibility The quality of being trustworthy and believable, said of a journalistic source.

editorial An article of opinion or interpretation.

feature story An article designed to entertain as well as to inform.

headline Type, usually 18 point or larger, used to introduce a story.

human interest story A type of story that focuses on individuals and how events or issues affect their life, generally offering a sense of relatability to the reader.

impartiality A principle of journalism that a story should not reflect a journalist's bias and should contain balance.

intention The motive or reason behind something, such as the publication of a news story.

motive The reason behind something, such as the publication of a news story or a source's perspective on an issue.

news story An article or style of expository writing that reports news, generally in a straightforward fashion and without editorial comment.

op-ed An opinion piece that reflects a prominent journalist's opinion on a topic of interest.

paraphrase The summary of an individual's words, with attribution, rather than a direct quotation of their exact words.

quotation The use of an individual's exact words, indicated by the use of quotation marks and proper attribution.

reliability The quality of being dependable and accurate, said of a journalistic source.

source The origin of the information reported in journalism.

tone A manner of expression in writing or speech.

Media Literacy Questions

1. In "Immigration Agency Rails Against Oakland Mayor's Warning of Raids" (on page 197), Thomas Fuller directly quotes Libby Schaaf. What are the strengths of the use of a direct quote as opposed to a paraphrase? What are its weaknesses?

2. Compare the headlines of "I.N.S. Ruling Benefits Illegal Immigrant Children" (on page 89) and "The Americans Left Behind by Deportation" (on page 119). Which is a more compelling headline, and why? How could the less compelling headline be changed to help better draw the reader's interest?

3. What type of story is "ICE Deportation Cases: Your Questions Answered" (on page 49)? Can you identify another article in this collection that is the same type of story?

4. The article "ICE Detained My Husband for Being an Activist" (on page 137) is an example of an op-ed. Identify how Amy Gottlieb's attitude, tone and perspective helps convey her opinion in the article.

5. Does "With Affluent Chinese Moving in, a Press War Begins to Heat Up" (on page 128) use multiple sources? What are the strengths of using multiple sources in a journalistic piece? What are the weaknesses of relying heavily on one source?

6. What is the intention of the article "Most Americans Want Legal Status for 'Dreamers.' These People Don't." (on page 114)? How effectively does it achieve its intended purpose?

7. The article "President Trump, How Is This Man a Danger?" (on page 140) is an example of an op-ed. Identify how Nicholas Kristof's attitude, tone and perspective help convey his opinion on the topic.

8. Often, as a news story develops, journalists' attitude toward the subject may change. Compare "Without New Laws or Walls, Trump Presses the Brake on Legal Immigration" (on page 176) and "Is America a 'Nation of Immigrants'? Immigration Agency Says No" (on page 189), both by Miriam Jordan. Did new information discovered between the publication of these two articles change Jordan's perspective?

9. Identify each of the sources in "For Elderly Immigrants, a Retirement Plan in U.S." (on page 25) as a primary source or a secondary source. Evaluate the reliability and credibility of each sources. How does your evaluation of each source change your perspective on this article?

10. Identify the various sources cited in the article "Working to Help Irish Immigrants Stay, Legally" (on page 123). How does the journalist attribute information to each of these sources in her article? How effective are her attributions in helping the reader identify her sources?

Citations

All citations in this list are formatted according to the Modern Language Association's (MLA) style guide.

BOOK CITATION

NEW YORK TIMES EDITORIAL STAFF, THE. *Immigration.* New York: New York Times Educational Publishing, 2019.

ONLINE ARTICLE CITATIONS

AGUILAR, JULIÁN. "Immigration; A Tale of Two Elections." *The New York Times,* 1 Jan. 2012, https://archive.nytimes.com/query.nytimes.com/gst/fullpage-9C02E2D7123CF932A35752C0A9649D8B63.html.

BENNER, KATIE, AND JENNIFER MEDINA. "Trump Administration Sues California Over Immigration Laws." *The New York Times,* 6 Mar. 2018, https://www.nytimes.com/2018/03/06/us/politics/justice-department-california-sanctuary-cities.html.

BONNER, RAYMOND. "New Policy Delays Visas for Specified Muslim Men." *The New York Times,* 10 Sept. 2002, http://www.nytimes.com/2002/09/10/world/threats-responses-immigration-new-policy-delays-visas-for-specified-muslim-men.html.

BROMWICH, JONAH ENGEL. "ICE Spokesman Resigns, Saying He Could No Longer Spread Falsehoods for Trump Administration." *The New York Times,* 13 Mar. 2018, https://www.nytimes.com/2018/03/13/us/california-ice-spokesman-resigns.html.

BUI, QUOCTRUNG, AND CAITLIN DICKERSON. "What Can the U.S. Learn From How Other Countries Handle Immigration?" *The New York Times,* 16 Feb. 2018, https://www.nytimes.com/interactive/2018/02/16/upshot/comparing-immigration-policies-across-countries.html.

CAVE, DAMIEN. "American Children, Now Struggling to Adjust to Life in Mexico." *The New York Times,* 18 Jun. 2012, http://www.nytimes.com/2012/06/19/world/americas/american-born-children-struggle-to-adjust-in-mexico.html.

CAVE, DAMIEN. "Better Lives for Mexicans Cut Allure of Going North." *The New York Times,* 6 Jul. 2011, http://www.nytimes.com/interactive/2011/07/06/world/americas/immigration.html.

CHEN, DAVID W. "With Affluent Chinese Moving In, a Press War Begins to Heat Up." *The New York Times,* 16 Apr. 1995, https://www.nytimes.com/1995/04/16/nyregion/immigration-with-affluent-chinese-moving-in-a-press-war-begins-to-heat-up.html.

CHOKSHI, NIRAJ, AND VIVIAN YEE. "ICE Deportation Cases: Your Questions Answered." *The New York Times,* 13 Feb. 2018, https://www.nytimes.com/2018/02/13/us/immigration-deportation-ice.html.

DICKERSON, CAITLIN. "For DACA Recipients, Losing Protection and Work Permits Is Just the Start." *The New York Times,* 7 Sept. 2017, https://www.nytimes.com/2017/09/07/us/daca-losses-immigration.html.

DICKSTEIN, SAMUEL. "Condemns Moves to Harass Aliens." *The New York Times,* 30 Jun. 1935, https://timesmachine.nytimes.com/timesmachine/1935/06/30/95508313.html?pageNumber=62.

DUGGER, CELIA W. "New Alliances and Attitudes on Aid." *The New York Times,* 1 Aug. 1997, http://www.nytimes.com/1997/08/01/us/new-alliances-and-attitudes-on-aid.html.

DUNN, ASHLEY. "For Elderly Immigrants, a Retirement Plan in U.S." *The New York Times,* 16 Apr. 1995, https://www.nytimes.com/1995/04/16/nyregion/for-elderly-immigrants-a-retirement-plan-in-us.html.

FERNANDEZ, MANNY. "Texas Banned 'Sanctuary Cities.' Some Police Departments Didn't Get the Memo." *The New York Times,* 15 Mar. 2018, https://www.nytimes.com/2018/03/15/us/texas-sanctuary-sb4-immigration.html.

FESSENDEN, FORD. "Mixed Scorecard for Immigrants' Children." *The New York Times,* 21 Oct. 2007, http://www.nytimes.com/2007/10/21/nyregion/nyregionspecial2/21immigrantnj.html.

FILES, JOHN. "Black Groups Seeking Asylum for a Teenager From Guinea." *The New York Times,* 14 Mar. 2004, https://www.nytimes.com/2004/03/14/us/black-groups-seeking-asylum-for-a-teenager-from-guinea.html.

FULLER, THOMAS. "Immigration Agency Rails Against Oakland Mayor's Warning of Raids." *The New York Times,* 28 Feb. 2018, https://www.nytimes.com/2018/02/28/us/oakland-mayor-ice-warning.html.

GOTTLIEB, AMY. "ICE Detained My Husband for Being an Activist." *The New York Times,* 18 Jan. 2018, https://www.nytimes.com/2018/01/18/opinion/ravi-ragbir-immigration-ice.html.

GREENHOUSE, STEVEN. "Safety Stings at Work Sites Will Be Halted." *The New York Times,* 29 Mar. 2006, http://www.nytimes.com/2006/03/29/politics/safety-stings-at-work-sites-will-be-halted.html.

HAAG, MATTHEW. "Former ICE Lawyer Pleads Guilty to Stealing Immigrants' Identities to Spend $190,000." *The New York Times,* 15 Feb. 2018, https://www.nytimes.com/2018/01/14/us/politics/daca-renewals-requests.html.

HABERMAN, MAGGIE, KATIE ROGERS, AND MICHAEL D. SHEAR. "Trump Says He Is Open to a Path to Citizenship for 'Dreamers'." *The New York Times,* 24 Jan. 2018, https://www.nytimes.com/2018/01/24/us/politics/trump-immigration-daca-dreamers-path-to-citizenship.html.

HAKIM, DANNY. "U.S. Official Is Indicted in Smuggling of Immigrants." *The New York Times,* 22 Apr. 2003, http://www.nytimes.com/2003/04/22/world/aftereffects-immigration-us-official-is-indicted-in-smuggling-of-immigrants.html.

HANDLIN, OSCAR. "Within the Gates." *The New York Times,* 19 Feb. 1950, https://www.nytimes.com/1950/02/19/archives/within-the-gates.html.

HOWE, MARVINE. "Employers Warned on Alien Hiring." *The New York Times,* 9 Aug. 1987, https://www.nytimes.com/1987/08/09/nyregion/employers-warned-on-alien-hiring.html.

HOWE, MARVINE. "I.N.S. Ruling Benefits Illegal Immigrant Children." *The New York Times,* 26 Mar. 1988, https://www.nytimes.com/1988/03/26/nyregion/ins-ruling-benefits-illegal-immigrant-children.html.

HOWE, MARVINE. "Working to Help Irish Immigrants Stay, Legally." *The New York Times,* 27 Nov. 1988, https://www.nytimes.com/1988/11/27/nyregion/working-to-help-irish-immigrants-stay-legally.html.

JORDAN, MIRIAM. "Did Melania Trump Merit an 'Einstein Visa'? Probably, Immigration Lawyers Say." *The New York Times,* 4 Mar. 2018, https://www.nytimes.com/2018/03/04/us/melania-trump-einstein-visa.html.

JORDAN, MIRIAM. "Is America a 'Nation of Immigrants'? Immigration Agency Says No." *The New York Times,* 22 Feb. 2018, https://www.nytimes.com/2018/02/22/us/uscis-nation-of-immigrants.html.

JORDAN, MIRIAM. "Most Americans Want Legal Status for 'Dreamers.' These People Don't." *The New York Times,* 25 Jan. 2018, https://www.nytimes.com/2018/01/25/us/dreamers-opponents-daca-deal.html.

JORDAN, MIRIAM. "Without New Laws or Walls, Trump Presses the Brake on Legal Immigration." *The New York Times,* 20 Dec. 2017, https://www.nytimes.com/2017/12/20/us/trump-immigration-slowdown.html.

KRISTOF, NICHOLAS. "President Trump, How Is This Man a Danger?" *The New York Times,* 10 Feb. 2018, https://www.nytimes.com/2018/02/10/opinion/sunday/syed-jamal-ice-deportation.html.

THE NEW YORK TIMES. "Don't Let the Amnesty Door Slam." *The New York Times,* 3 Nov. 1987, https://www.nytimes.com/1987/11/03/opinion/don-t-let-the-amnesty-door-slam.html.

THE NEW YORK TIMES. "Illegal Aliens' Health — and Ours." *The New York Times,* 10 Aug. 1986, https://www.nytimes.com/1986/08/10/opinion/illegal-aliens-health-and-ours.html.

THE NEW YORK TIMES. "Immigration." *The New York Times,* 26 Aug. 1890, https://timesmachine.nytimes.com/timesmachine/1890/08/26/103261902.html?pageNumber=4.

THE NEW YORK TIMES. "The Immigration Debate; A Nation of Laws and of Immigrants." *The New York Times,* 16 May 2006, https://www.nytimes.com/2006/05/16/us/the-immigration-debate-a-nation-of-laws-and-of-immigrants.html.

PEAR, ROBERT. "Court Ruling May Open Way for More Political Refugees." *The New York Times,* 15 Mar. 1987, https://www.nytimes.com/1987/03/15/weekinreview/immigration-policy-court-ruling-may-open-way-for-more-political-refugees.html.

PRESTON, JULIA. "Pink Slips at Disney. But First, Training Foreign Replacements." *The New York Times,* 3 Jun. 2015, https://www.nytimes.com/2015/06/04/us/last-task-after-layoff-at-disney-train-foreign-replacements.html.

ROBBINS, LIZ. "Activists and ICE Face Off Over Detained Immigrant Leader." *The New York Times,* 12 Jan. 2018, https://www.nytimes.com/2018/01/12/nyregion/immigration-activist-deportation.html.

ROBBINS, LIZ. "At Least 1,900 Immigrants Were Rejected Because of Mail Problems." *The New York Times,* 5 Jan. 2018, https://www.nytimes.com/2018/01/05/nyregion/mail-problems-daca-denial-of-work-permits-for-1900-immigrants.html.

ROBBINS, LIZ. "Once Routine, Immigration Check-Ins Are Now High Stakes." *The New York Times,* 11 Apr. 2017, https://www.nytimes.com/2017/04/11/nyregion/ice-immigration-check-in-deportation.html.

ROBBINS, LIZ, AND MIRIAM JORDAN. "Fearing DACA's Return May Be Brief, Immigrants Rush to Renew." *The New York Times,* 16 Jan. 2018, https://www.nytimes.com/2018/01/16/nyregion/renew-daca-immigration-permits.html.

ROHTER, LARRY. "Mexico Fears the Loss of America as a Safety Valve." *The*

New York Times, 15 Mar. 1987, https://www.nytimes.com/1987/03/15/week-inreview/immigration-policy-mexico-fears-the-loss-of-america-as-a-safety-valve.html.

SANTORA, MARC. "'08 Candidates Weighing Consequences as They Take Sides on Immigration Plan." *The New York Times,* 19 May 2007, http://www.nytimes.com/2007/05/19/us/politics/19candidates.html.

SCHMITT, ERIC. "U.S. Will Seek to Fingerprint Visas' Holders." *The New York Times,* 5 Jun. 2002, http://www.nytimes.com/2002/06/05/us/traces-of-terror-immigration-us-will-seek-to-fingerprint-visas-holders.html.

STEVENS, MATT. "DACA Participants Can Again Apply for Renewal, Immigration Agency Says." *The New York Times,* 14 Jan. 2018, https://www.nytimes.com/2018/01/14/us/politics/daca-renewals-requests.html.

SWARNS, RACHEL L. "Republican Split on Immigration Reflects Nation's Struggle." *The New York Times,* 29 Mar. 2006, http://www.nytimes.com/2006/03/29/us/republican-split-on-immigration-reflects-nations-struggle.html.

SWARNS, RACHEL L. "U.N. Report Cites Harassment of Immigrants Who Sought Asylum at American Airports." *The New York Times,* 13 Aug. 2004, https://www.nytimes.com/2004/08/13/world/threats-responses-immigration-un-report-cites-harassment-immigrants-who-sought.html.

SWARNS, RACHEL L. "U.S. to Give Border Patrol Agents the Power to Deport Illegal Aliens." *The New York Times,* 11 Aug. 2004, http://www.nytimes.com/2004/08/11/world/threats-responses-immigration-us-give-border-patrol-agents-power-deport-illegal.html.

THOMPSON-HERNÁNDEZ, WALTER. "How One Sport Is Keeping a Language, and a Culture, Alive." *The New York Times,* 13 Mar. 2018, https://www.nytimes.com/2018/03/13/sports/pelota-mixteca-mexican-culture-sports.html.

VILLAVICENCIO, KARLA CORNEJO. "The Americans Left Behind by Deportation." *The New York Times,* 28 Feb. 2018, https://www.nytimes.com/2018/02/28/opinion/american-families-immigrants-deportation.html.

Index

A

Aguilar, Julián, 71
Alcaide Eligio, Marcela, 105, 108–109
American dream, 8, 26, 121
amnesty, 23–24, 90, 114–118, 124–125, 165–166
Arizona, 61, 64, 71, 83, 96
asylum, 35–36, 38–41, 51, 53, 131–132, 143–146, 175, 190
attitudes toward immigration
   in late 19th century, 11–12
   in 1930s, 13–15
   in 1950s, 16–17
   in 1980s, 18–19, 20–22, 23–24, 89–91, 123–127, 143–146
   in 1990s, 25–30, 147–150
Australia, 184–185, 187

B

Benner, Katie, 201–205
Berrones, Jesus, 49–50, 52
Blando, Steve, 99–100
Bonner, Raymond, 154–156
Bonner, Robert C., 39–40
Bromwich, Jonah Engel, 206–208
Brown, Jerry, 201, 202
Bui, Quoctrung, 183–188
Bush, George W., 64, 161–166
Bush administration, 151, 154–155

C

California, 80, 107, 197–200, 201–205
Canada, 34, 38, 184–185, 187
Cave, Damien, 60–70, 72–78
chain migration, 111, 112, 115, 187, 195
check-ins for immigrants, 138, 170–175
Chen, David W., 128–130
children and immigration, 89–91, 92–93, 94–98, 99–101, 102–104, 105–109, 110–113, 114–118, 119–122
Chinese immigrants, 128–130
Chokshi, Niraj, 49–53
Clinton, Bill, 64, 147, 148, 149
Clinton, Hillary Rodham, 167–168
Collins, Jeffrey G., 31, 32
Corcoran, Richard, 86–87
Cotton, Tom, 111

D

Deferred Action for Childhood Arrivals (DACA), 94–98, 99–101, 102–104, 105–109, 110–113, 114–118
de la Madrid, Miguel, 57
deportation, 13–15, 34–37, 38–41, 49–53, 56–59, 61, 72–75, 77–78, 119–122, 145, 165–166, 170–172

detention, 51, 120, 131–132, 133–136, 137–139, 140–142
Dickerson, Caitlin, 94–98, 183–188
Dickstein, Samuel, 13–15
Dream Act, 98, 111
Dreamers. See Deferred Action for Childhood Arrivals (DACA)
Dugger, Celia W., 147–150
Dunn, Ashley, 25–30
Durbin, Richard J., 111

E

EB-1 visa ("Einstein visa"), 192–196
Einstein, Albert, 10, 193–194
elderly immigrants 25–30
employers and undocumented workers, 20–22, 23
   fines for hiring, 21, 56
English language requirement, 166
European Union, 185

F

Fernandez, Manny, 85–88
Fessenden, Ford, 92–93
Files, John, 131–132
fines for hiring undocumented workers, 21, 56
fingerprinting, 151–153, 165
Fossil (watchmaker), 45–46

Fuller, Thomas, 197–200

G

Ghedini, Joung-ah, 39, 41
Giuliani, Rudolph W., 147, 167–168
Gonzalez, Amparo, 94, 98
González, Graciela Treviño, 77
Gottlieb, Amy, 133–136, 137–139
Graham, Lindsey, 111, 159
green cards, 70, 101, 117, 120, 121–122, 137, 151, 176, 181–182, 190, 192–196
Greenhouse, Steven, 42
Gulf states, 186–187

H

Haag, Matthew, 54–55
Haberman, Maggie, 110–113
Hakim, Danny, 31–33
Halstead, Janice, 31–32, 33
Handlin, Oscar, 16–17
health care and undocumented immigrants, 18–19
Hernandez, Mario, 106
Hira, Ronil, 44, 45
Homan, Thomas D., 197, 198, 199, 203, 204, 206, 207
H-1B visa, 43–48, 177–181
Howe, Marvine, 20–22, 89–91, 123–127
H-2A visa, 68–70
Hutchinson, Asa, 35, 36, 131, 132

I

illegal immigrants. *See* undocumented immigrants
Illegal Immigration and Reform Responsibility Act (1996), 34
immigrants
asylum, 35–36, 38–41, 51, 53, 131–132, 143–146, 190
children, 89–91, 92–93, 94–98, 99–101, 102–104, 105–109, 110–113, 114–118, 119–122
Chinese, 128–130
elderly, 25–30
fingerprinting, 151–153, 165
illegal. *See* undocumented immigrants
immigration check-ins, 138, 170–175
Irish, 123–127
Muslim, 111, 131–132, 151, 154–156, 170, 176
notable, 9–10, 142, 192–196
number in United States, 8, 13–14, 157, 158
requirement to speak English, 166
smuggling, 31–33
temporary worker program, 164–165, 168–169
welfare, 18–19, 25–30, 147–150
Immigration and Customs Enforcement (I.C.E.), 42, 49–53, 120, 133–136, 137–139, 172–175, 197–200, 206–208
Immigration and Naturalization Service (I.N.S.), 20–22, 23–24, 89–91, 132, 144, 153
Immigration Reform and Control Act (1986), 20–22, 23–24, 89–90
immigration to United States
in late 19th century, 11–12, 150
in 1920s-1930s, 13–15, 63
in 1950s-1960s, 16–17, 63
in 1980s, 18–19, 20–22, 23–24, 56–59, 89–91, 123–127, 143–146
in 1990s, 25–30, 147–150
chain migration, 111, 112, 115, 187, 195
compared to other countries, 183–188
green cards, 70, 101, 117, 120, 121–122, 137, 151, 176, 181–182, 190, 192–196
by lottery, 104, 112, 117, 125–126, 177–178
merit based, 104, 115, 184–185, 187–188, 192–196
naturalization, 13, 16, 89, 149–150, 191
open border policy, 8, 16
quotas, 8, 11, 12, 15, 16–17
reform, 183–188, 189–191
Republican views on, 157–160, 161–166
temporary worker program, 164–165, 168–169
I-9 forms, 21–22
Irish immigrants, 123–127
Isidoro family, 72, 73–75, 77–78

J

Jacoma, Amelia, 28
Jamal, Syed Ahmed, 49–50, 52–53, 140–142
Japan, 185–186
Jarno, Malik, 131–132
Jordan, Miriam, 105–109,

114–118, 176–182, 189–191, 192–196

K
Kerr bill, 14, 15
Kristof, Nicholas, 140–142

L
lottery, 104, 112, 117, 125–126, 177–178

M
MacCormack, Daniel W., 13–14
Matloff, Norman S., 26–27, 29
McCain, John, 167
McKeon, Edward, 62, 68–69
Medicaid, 18–19
Medina, Jennifer, 201–205
merit-based immigration, 104, 115, 184–185, 187–188, 192–196
Mexico, 34, 38, 60–70, 72–75, 77–78, 119
  border security, 64, 110, 162–164
  reverse migration, 56–59
  2012 presidential election, 71
Muslims and immigration, 111, 131–132, 151, 154–156, 170, 176

N
National Guard, 163
"nation of immigrants, a," 157, 161–162, 189–191
naturalization, 13, 16, 89, 149–150, 191
New Jersey, 92–93, 128–130
New York Times, The, 11–12, 18–19, 23–24, 161–166

Noroña, Mauricio, 99
Northeast Utilities, 46
notable immigrants, 9–10, 192–196
number of immigrants in United States, 8, 13–14, 157, 158

O
Oakland, Calif., raid, 197–200, 204, 206–207
Obama, Barack, 64, 71, 98, 102, 169
Obama administration, 52, 74, 122, 141–142, 181, 200
O'Malley, John, 20, 21, 22
open border policy, 8, 16
Orozco family, 60, 62, 63–64, 65, 66–67, 70

P
Pear, Robert, 143–146
pelota mixteca, 79–80, 82–84
Perez, Denia, 97, 98
Pham, Huy, 114, 117, 118
political refugees, 38–41, 131–132, 143–146
Preston, Julia, 43–48

Q
quotas, 8, 11, 12, 15, 16–17

R
Ragbir, Ravi, 133–136, 137–139, 174
Reagan, Ronald, 116, 126, 144
reform efforts, 183–188, 189–191
Republican views on immigration, 157–160, 161–166
Robbins, Liz, 99–101,

105–109, 133–136, 170–175
Rogers, Katie, 110–113
Rohter, Larry, 56–59

S
Saenz, Thomas A., 87, 96
Sanchez, Raphael A., 54–55
sanctuary cities/states, 85–88, 112, 113, 197–200, 201–205
Santora, Marc, 167–169
Schaaf, Libby, 197–200, 204, 206, 207
Schmitt, Eric, 151–153
Schwab, James, 198, 200, 206–208
Sessions, Jeff, 112–113, 116, 202–203, 206
Shear, Michael D., 110–113
Southern California Edison, 45
South Korea, 185–186
Stein, Daniel, 26, 97–98, 172
Sterry, Pav, 114, 115, 118
Stevens, John Paul, 144
Stevens, Matt, 102–104
sting operations and undocumented immigrants, 42
Supplemental Security Income (S.S.I.), 25–30, 147, 148, 149
Swarns, Rachel L., 34–37, 38–41, 157–160

T
temporary worker program, 164–165, 168–169
Texas, 71, 85–88, 96
Thompson-Hernández, Walter, 79–80, 82–84

Tienda, Marta, 73, 78
Trump, Donald J., 94, 98, 102, 103–104, 110–113, 115–116, 140, 170, 171, 183, 184–185, 195
  Trump administration, 50, 52, 101, 102, 103, 107, 110–113, 120, 121, 176–182, 190, 197–200, 201–205, 206–208
Trump, Melania, 142, 192–196
2008 presidential election, 167–169

U

undocumented immigrants
  amnesty, 23–24, 90, 124–125
  children, 89–91, 94–98, 99–101, 102–104, 105–109, 110–113, 114–118, 119–122
  deportation, 13–15, 34–37, 38–41, 49–53, 56–59, 61, 72–75, 77–78, 119–122, 145, 165–166, 170–172
  detention, 51, 120, 131–132, 133–136, 137–139, 140–142
  employers, 20–22, 23
  fines for hiring, 21, 56
  health care, 18–19
  immigration check-ins, 138, 170–175
  raid in Oakland, Calif., 197–200, 204, 206–207
  sanctuary cities/states, 85–88, 112, 113, 197–200, 201–205
  sting operations, 42
  welfare, 18–19, 26
United Nations, 38–39, 40
U.S. Border Patrol, 34–37, 38–41, 162–164
U.S. Citizenship and Immigration Services (U.S.C.I.S.), 99–101, 102–104, 105, 107, 178, 189–191, 193–196
U.S. Department of Homeland Security, 34–37, 38–41, 42, 132, 143, 198

V

Vásquez, Rafael, 80, 82
Villavicencio, Karla Cornejo, 119–122
visas, 154–156, 176, 190
  EB-1 ("Einstein visa"), 192–196
  fingerprinting, 151–153
  H-1B, 43–48, 177–181
  H-2A, 68–70

W

Walt Disney World, 43, 45, 46–48, 177
welfare, 18–19, 26

Y

Yee, Vivian, 49–53

Z

Zúñiga, Víctor, 72, 77

$53.26

LONGWOOD PUBLIC LIBRARY
800 Middle Country Road
Middle Island, NY 11953
(631) 924-6400
longwoodlibrary.org

LIBRARY HOURS

Monday-Friday	9:30 a.m. - 9:00 p.m.
Saturday	9:30 a.m. - 5:00 p.m.
Sunday (Sept-June)	1:00 p.m. - 5:00 p.m.